AN

ITALIAN

JOURNEY

AN

ITALIAN

JOURNEY

❦

J E A N   G I O N O

Translated from the French by John Cumming

ᵀＭᴾ

THE MARLBORO PRESS/NORTHWESTERN
NORTHWESTERN UNIVERSITY PRESS
EVANSTON, ILLINOIS

The Marlboro Press/Northwestern
Northwestern University Press
Evanston, Illinois 60208-4210

Printed in the United States of America

ISBN 0-8101-6027-7

Library of Congress Cataloging-in-Publication Data

Giono, Jean, 1895–1970.
    [Voyage en Italie. English]
    An Italian journey / Jean Giono ; translated from the French by
John Cumming.
      p. cm.
    ISBN 0-8101-6027-7 (alk. paper)
    1. Giono, Jean, 1895–1970—Journeys—Italy. 2. Authors,
French—20th century—Journeys—Italy. 3. Italy—Description and
travel. I. Cumming, John, 1937– . II. Title.
PQ2613.I57Z475513 1998
914.504'924—dc21   98-34123
                                                    CIP

CONTENTS

Setting Out

I am not a traveler, I assure you. I seem scarcely to have moved in fifty years. I was forced to earn my own living at an early age. When I was fifteen I started in a bank at twenty francs a month, and began to observe the wholly common run of human emotions. I became a spectator at a never-ending rehearsal, at a door that opened on truth. Others, however, were closed to me. Though my father had bequeathed me much more than the usual degree of imaginative insight, I found it neither unfair nor improper to be asked to look at things sensibly and logically. So I organized my life and began to enjoy looking for the cause behind the effect.

I wasn't vain then, nor am I now. I quite humbly accept all challenges to examine and even marvel at what I find around me. I stayed at the bank not for a few days or months but for twenty years. My present and my future depended entirely on the inspector who monitored my work from time to time. He was a stout man with a beard, a cigar smoker who never made any effort to hide his contempt for the vacant look I owed to my blue eyes. I might well have been a first-class employee, as he recognized, but he always kept me on a tightrope. This put me in a continual state of dread and wariness.

Nevertheless, I recall that period of my lifetime with great pleasure. Everything, in the end, was for the good. It is very helpful to run the risk of being reduced to penury from the start of your life. Only just managing to rub along is enough to make the most apprehensive of creatures (and I am certainly one of them) feel he or she has won a famous victory. That can be very beneficial and even enjoyable after a time (though, of course, it's essential to know how to put on the right sort of front). I met that inspector again in 1934 (he died, I think, in 1938). He asked me to inscribe a copy of one of my books for him, and I wrote something very affectionate in it. He still scared me, but I realized that he was entangled in his own needs and, like everyone else, incapable of being either very good or very bad.

Fear, then, had deprived me of any urge to travel. Eventually, I found that I was sensitive enough to experience some minor pleasures and even major delights in that dark office where we had to light the lamps around midday. Nothing was so pleasurable as those long, rainy winter days when I was dry, warm, and with time enough to consider what I really wanted. After all, I was very lucky to have somewhere to sit, where I could earn twenty francs. Anyone, surely, would have agreed that leaving would have been more than rash.

Of course I was far too inclined to let sentiment interfere with things. But there were so many responsibilities about which nothing need be said (but which weigh you down when you are sixteen), and duties I was anxious to fulfill. At that time my father, already an old man, had become willfully reticent. My love for him made me all the more alarmed when I heard him talking to his invisible partner. I wanted to make sure that he enjoyed a happy old age, if only by not having to rely on him. But all that depended on the half-Havana enthusiast. On Sunday evenings I used to pass by the bank building to reassure myself that it had not vanished during my short walks in the hills. You don't abandon habits like that if they take hold of you at a very tender age. To think of all the things I substituted for that cigar smoker when I had what people call freedom! Anything could take his place. Hence what seemed like an attachment to a specific area and even love for a certain way of life.

And so I had been thinking for three or four years that a visit to Italy was necessary, yet put it off from one day to the next. Finally I had my passport made out. That did not commit me to anything. The document had been lying on the table for a long time, but now it was in my pocket. We would soon be on our way. Our friends Antoine and Germaine were driving us there.

Standing in front of my table gave me an odd feeling. It wasn't a workplace any longer. I had put the top on the inkwell and the pens away, and my papers were filed.

Fortunately I had to solve a minor problem right away. The Renault 4 HP convertible (converted indeed, for the roof had been folded back) we were using could hold only a limited amount of luggage. My wife and I had just one small suitcase, but as we were going by way of Mont-Genèvre we needed our coats. Then it was autumn, the light was russet-gold, the rain would soon be coming, and we had to find room in the car for all sorts of gear. I had also stuffed my notebook, maps, a guidebook, and another book into a beach bag, and I wanted to make sure that all these "impedimenta" were within reach. In the end, I fitted the bag in by my feet (we were in the back seat) and managed to stow capes and raincoats under the folded roof. We left abruptly after giving

Sylvie a little kiss and saying goodbye to Fine. I had the feeling that my wife hadn't given Fine sufficiently detailed instructions about running the house when we were away. In short, our departure was like leaving for a picnic in the neighboring countryside, or when I spent a few days at Antoine's at Gréoulx, about eleven kilometers away. I could hardly believe that I was really on my way to Italy (but then I might as well have been leaving for Tibet).

Of course I know the landscape around Manosque very well. After all, I was born there. I don't always feel I am going away when I drive along the roads that I cycle on to visit my farm. Neither twenty nor thirty nor even forty kilometers can take me away from my usual surroundings.

I haven't left home at all when I go through Lurs, Peyruis, or Saint-Auban. Now we were making for the Alps, and even that route was quite reassuring. I am at home in the mountains. I hate and detest the sea. At Manosque I always walk in an easterly direction so that, at the bend in the hills where the valley of the Durance opens out, I suddenly come upon the Alps: vast sugar lumps piled up in the blue immensity of an opalescent bowl.

My blood is aroused, and I breathe headily at the mere sight of glaciers and chamois pastures. I never look over to the southwest, to Marseilles and the sea, a ghastly expanse of sandpaper rasping bodies and souls, and eroding even the rocks. (Oceans, to be sure, may have the same properties as mountains, but my means will take me into the Alps though not onto the high seas. In this respect, as so often, I have always had to travel on the cheap.) When my daughter Aline was little we used to spend the height of summer in the mountains, at Saint-Julien-en-Beauchêne; and when my other daughter, Sylvie, was very young, we would go to

Briançon from July to October. I have always found it uplifting to walk along with the mountains stretching up before me.

This was partly why I chose the Mont-Genèvre route. If you reach Italy by sea you get there flayed alive. You have to hug the vulgarity of the entire Côte d'Azur, and then follow the west and east Riviera all the way around the Gulf of Genoa. That means much too much sandpaper and grated cheese, and all those kilometers of women in the buff. I was not going to take off (after so many precautions) in order to see Le Trayas or Cannes. First I needed the resounding empty spaces that come before the mountains; then to ascend and finally breathe that limpid, silvery air and survey those brown expanses. I have always hated crowds. I like deserts, prisons, and monasteries. I have discovered, too, that there are fewer idiots at three thousand meters above sea level than down below. (This, plainly, is the attitude of a fifty-seven-year-old man who has remained shy and scarcely adept at paying compliments, though as regretfully as that threefold condition implies.) Nothing makes me begin to feel happier than the avenues leading into the Alps. Then my eyes glow like the windows of a country cottage when the lamps are lighted.

As luck would have it, the clear and sparkling weather we had enjoyed in the low valley became overlaid—with expectation too, for some corners of the sky between two summits were even turning storm-black. I imagined Mont-Genèvre thick with heavy mists, and pleasurably anticipated reaching the other side as the car all but hastened there. At times the poplar and aspen leaves were already golden. These trees seemed so melancholy against the dark sky. They formed a royal escort of alabaster trunks at the entry to Embrun. We all agreed to keep the roof drawn back in spite of the menacing weather. Then we could watch the high Briançon landscape coalesce around us.

In 1934–35 Elise and I had been supremely happy in this area. We had rented four big rooms from a Madame Dumont at the hamlet of Les Queyrelles. They were in an enormous house that looked like a monastery. We were opposite the town of Briançon, and only slightly above it, yet sufficiently high up to look down on the ramparts and gateways that made it like a view in an old engraving. I sat in the orchard enclosed by walls that gave the house the air of a secluded Carthusian monastery. I found this especially appealing. I watched the loaded mules passing over the drawbridges beside black peasant and blue soldier figures. The mountain beeches came down in a throng, all the way to the public fountain where we went to collect the water for soup. Immediately below us we heard the gentle rumbling of the Clarée and its confluence with the Durance. The nights were cradled by the sound of the waters moving over those still attractive slopes. Just before dawn the wind from Lautaret began to raise the murmuring from the poplars above that of the mountain stream. We started every morning with Bach's Brandenburg Concertos on the gramophone. Some good friends would arrive to share our meals. My friend Lucien Jacques, the painter, was staying with us (afterward he and I used to go to the meadows to gather those little pink mushrooms in their fairy rings; after eating them we suffered from quite disturbing hallucinations that seized us when we were awake). I worked in a dark and resonant attic with hauntingly large pieces of furniture like none I have ever known elsewhere, though the vast lectern had its uses. Aline, serious yet delicate, profited from her Italianate features to charm the birds in the orchard into childhood friendships (which she also set up with the ants and rose chafers). Sylvie, plump and beautiful in her cradle, could only flourish on her surfeit of milk. Elise broke her ankle one morning when we were camping in the vineyard at Cavalles.

We recognized the place where we had stayed then. Now and again roofs would poke their noses through the leaves to inspect us. We craned our necks to see them.

As we reached the heights of Briançon and arrived at the Champ-de-Mars, an icy wind attacked us from ahead. Before us the slopes that we had to ascend on our way to the pass were covered with clouds, and a moderate sleet from the light veil drifting in the valley began to patter on our windshield.

It was on the same Champ-de-Mars that I first learned to be a soldier, in February 1915. I had been drafted as a recruit into the 159th Infantry Regiment in barracks at Briançon. Later, before leaving for the front, I had mounted guard for a month at Fort Infernet. When the weather was good I could see the yellow fog in the east that was Piedmont. An old artillery sergeant from the fortress persuaded us that some plumes of smoke were actually Turin. My father had often told me about Turin. His family was from Montezemolo in Piedmont. Even in 1951 I found those words especially captivating. For me they meant something other than what they generally evoke. They were redolent of the Grand'rue in 1907 and, more particularly, of the immense, supposedly gloomy house where we lived in that narrow street. There were shops there, of course, but it was very close to alleyways lined with sheep byres and with stables where they kept the horses that pulled the buses. At that time, too, I loved the scent of linenette and the steam from women's underwear when my mother was ironing. I shall say nothing of the universally prevailing smell of leather in our house. The sergeant at Fort Infernet (his name was Bec, I think) had no inkling of the sad associations he aroused in me when he mentioned Piedmont and Turin. I had arrived in a state bordering much more on homesickness than that of the other conscripts, except perhaps for four or five peasants, but they only felt strongly about the earth, which, after all, was there too, under their feet. From their first days in the barracks, they showed an interest in the local fairs, where they went to discuss the price of sheep and of pork on the hoof. That was in 1915. One day one of them called Saille, who was wounded near me at Verdun later on, went all the way to Embrun where he had been told there was a very big cattle market, especially for goats. It was in Briançon castle barracks and, more precisely, in the recess of the second-floor window overlooking Asfeld bridge, that I developed a taste for not owning, for not having, for being deprived of essential things such as freedom, and even the freedom to live. I remember incising something to that effect in the stone up there. I don't know exactly what I wrote, but I can still see myself scratching away with my knifepoint, on the whole quite pleased to be doing it. From that point, before that severe landscape, I date my tendency to avoid excess or, rather, my compulsion to lose out.

Now, on the banks of the road we were following up to the pass, I was looking out for clusters of the tiny blue gentians that had given me so much joy in 1915. But it was too late in the season. Now, like the foxes, the fields of Mount Genèvre were already in their winter coats. It was cold, and the thick haze had reached out to moisten our cheeks. Still, we did not close the hood, but only because we hoped to be able to dive swiftly into Italy on the other side.

We had to stop at the first barrier at the frontier to prove that we were innocent travelers. We could hear the stove roaring in the little house where the border guard kept his rubber stamps. All that was needed to incite our sympathy was the hot air on our frozen knees. I have never liked a representative of law and order so much as this one, as he applied his various stamps to the pages of our passports. I wanted him to start questioning us, and to do so as meticulously as possible. I hoped there would be many, many points to elucidate; that he would begin to knit his blond brows; and even that he would imprison us in this wonderfully hot place. His wife was knitting away very agreeably before the window and near the stove. How lucky she was to be a policeman's wife and to knit at a certain spot (and a comfortable one in the bargain). We weren't so fortunate. We had to go on to Italy. The sleet on the windowsill of the border post sounded like wine fermenting.

One kilometer further down we came to the customs post, in a hamlet that was already Italian.

II

Turin, Milan, Brescia

Of course I had not undertaken this journey for the mere pleasure of going somewhere else. There is a kind of enjoyment that does not depend on anyone or on the countryside. It is the pleasure that I have always sought for. Three or four hundred kilometers more to the east or to the west, a thousand even, and it would be the same. Perhaps this will explain it. For more than twenty years I had been reading and rereading Machiavelli. Don't think that I wanted to be a dictator or a democrat. I was merely a man with a pet subject. I enjoyed reading Machiavelli and went on doing so. That took me on to the *Novellieri*, to Guicciardini, Vettori, then Pignotti, Sismondi, Potter, Tanburini, and so on. In short, I was often in Tuscany, the Romagna, Lombardy, and Venice. But since I did not know these regions, I had to see them with the eyes of faith. This trip would enable me to see them quite physically.

Then there was my famous grandfather. He died fifty years before I was born, to the very day. He was born in March 1795, and I in March 1895. There was exactly a century between us. But I had been interested in him for a long time. Deeply interested. When I was seventeen, I would go up the stairs of our dark old house, which was full of hiding places and of nooks and corners where, at any minute, I expected to see the mustachioed Piedmontese companions of this revolutionary brigand jump out, rolling their eyes and grinding their teeth. All I carried was one of those little petrol lamps with a tiny glass funnel. It trembled in its metal recess as I shivered like a leaf. I was looking for my father in his studio. There the old *Carbonaro* came to life. Together with him, and for my sake, my father had constructed a vast oral novel. Every evening they added episodes packed with picaresque details. This was like a bag of sugar candy pure and simple. I could never have enough. I have always adored this unprincipled rogue. His sole virtue, however impregnated it may have been by the attitude of 1848, the year of revolutions, was his belief that liberty was the gateway to the happiness of the greatest number. I owe my naive principles to him. Moreover, he had knocked around Piedmont, Lombardy, the Romagna, Tuscany, and Venetia. No doubt I would come across him there too.

I had imagined a Turin very different from the reality. I had heard of its long straight streets with orderly intersections and right-angled corners, a whole area of quadrilaterals. I had expected a modern city. But I found an old capital.

In spite of the fine drizzle that first evening in Turin, Elise and I went for a walk along the Via Garibaldi. We were in a state very close to perfect happiness. There was no trace of the need to affect boredom that produced such petrified creatures elsewhere. Even pretty women were interested in everything around them. They were obviously happy just to be out. I hardly had occasion there to wonder why they looked so sad when they were enjoying themselves. I realized that in Turin you could still afford the luxury of being overtly romantic. There seemed to be no such thing as public opinion but only personal opinions. That was also evident from the rather quaint soldiers you came across, in battle dress, yes, but with a little touch of Paolo Uccello in a beret here, in the sleeves there, and in epaulets here and there.

The population of Turin was almost equivalent to that of Marseilles yet there was no trace of vulgarity, for it had been a capital city. What is more, it had been a capital with a king and tyrant, whereas the only tyranny that Marseilles had suffered was the rule of trade and of bank accounts. In Turin, at the least sign of individuality in your behavior they omitted the commercial court and brought you before a supreme court clad in scarlet and designed to issue death sentences. To be outside the law there meant wearing gray, but in Marseilles all it meant was that you were insolvent: in other words, that you were not wickedly cunning. In Turin it was very difficult to endure the derisory condition of not knowing how to make money. Anything was better than that, even naked, groveling meanness. You could see all this in people's eyes.

Perhaps I saw too much in an hour's walk. When you are happy you should look on the best side of things. I am not a tourist, or rather I am also one when I stroll around my garden. The only account I want to give has to do with feelings. Globe-trotters and wits have said everything else that can be said.

I walked past the famous right angles. They revealed dark prospects sparsely dotted with occasional lights. I could see the colonnades. The transverse streets were deserted; I could people them as I wished. For instance, I could easily imagine my grandfather there, hugging the walls.

These were the kind of streets that Angelo (a character in one of my novels, *The Horseman on the Roof*) entered on the sweet-tempered horse he bought at Théus, after crossing a cholera-ridden France. He passed through its arcades. He was in the right place at last: in other words, he no longer had to choose between five or six ways of dealing with the dangers that faced him, when each strategy seemed more appealing than any other. He thought: "The only fever here is an epidemic of freedom. All I have to do is to reach the other side of the barricade. I don't have to play nurse any longer, as with the young woman I managed to save in the end."

Birds fighting in the trees awakened me early that morning. I went onto the balcony. My bedroom looked out on the Corso Francia. The sky was still overcast, but it was very mild outside. The sun rising over the roofs was already touching the clouds with red. I was one floor above a bus station where people were waiting. They were probably office workers and typists on their way to the Rivoli factories. They were no noisier than the birds, but noisy for all that. There was no sign as yet of those ridiculous motorcycles like so many commodes on which their riders farted acceptably through the traffic, or that carried men with leather briefcases. From the side of the Piazza di Statuto you could detect a horse trotting over the cobbles and the sound of ironbound cartwheels. A basketmaker, a rag-and-bone man, or a rabbit-skin seller blew on a little trumpet and occasionally added a neatly synchronized cry to the horse's rhythmic trotting. The noise of the trolleybus that eventually bore my typists away was hardly more noticeable than a cat purring. This was the time when, now and then, you could hear a city's trees.

We had got to know the coffee everyone talked of. It was drawn off in a thin stream from a vast still that sputtered like an ancient railway engine. Admittedly, I was at the hotel bar just when these great machines were adjusted. Engineers were needed for this task. In this case, the expert was a valet who gave instructions to a girl. She manipulated handles and turned wheels, the tubing shook, steam spurted from all the joints, and the cylinders seemed about to yield some marvel or monster. I should have imitated the attitude of the acolytes about the device, for they remained quite undaunted, as if to show that nothing unusual was afoot. By their ministrations, however, they managed to suppress the coffee's aroma, which is so enjoyable in the morning. I found this a great loss. It is not so much drinking coffee as feeling that you are about to do so that I like. Nevertheless, I smoked my first pipe of the day with pleasure.

We planned to whisk away to Milan, where I had to see a friend, then to leave the city out and to get to the Venice area as soon as possible. Bergamo or Brescia, I thought, but Antoine told us he had a headache. That would change everything. Still, I wanted to get close to the mountains, and the map showed me that the road went in that direction after Milan. Before leaving we drove around Turin. This bore out my impressions of the night before. These streets without pavements but flagged with great stones were operas in themselves. All was trade and industry. So many years of habitually expressing the emotions had decided the design of the set. It was quite permissible to display feeling and sensitivity without fear of scorn, and the builders had taken advantage of this. My old façades in the Via Garibaldi, the Via Pô, and the Piazza Vittorio Veneto were not beautiful, but you felt that behind them you could stage a play if you wanted, and that is a good feeling. How odd, I thought, to come across Shakespeare here at every step. The evening before I had already seen dramatic thresholds, doors, alleyways, and arcades fit even for *Richard III*. Yet this was only Turin, which is never mentioned in this respect.

At the Victor Emmanuel Bridge you are in the shadow of a high black hill. Here you are not reminded of occasions in history as such. Instead, at every moment the appearance of things teases out your own personal story. So many times the greenery of those dark depths, rococo monasteries, and art-nouveau villas emerging from pine thickets had already played their sad parts in my heart. We went along the Via Roma because the book said we should, but there was nothing to it but fine shops. We entered squares centered on very weird bronze statues. It was always the same man, dressed like a cashier at the Banque de France or in the ornate uniform of a member of the French Academy. He was on horseback, though sometimes he was galloping and sometimes quite still yet brandishing his little sword. The most astonishing pose was when he had come a cropper and his horse was waving its hooves in the air. Only a certain attitude to life enables you to make a statue of a monarch in that condition.

For two days now it had been decided that we would not forgo the pleasure of taking the *autostrada*. The marked route that was taking us toward this superhighway went through areas that I was beginning once again to find attractive. These were broad streets lined with low houses. The sun smiled every now and then, and the rough-cast walls were turning yellow. There were no caryatids here or old coats of arms, but rough-cast walls as only a good Piedmontese mason can make them. It was a pleasure to see them. The lime was applied so that it drank up the light. From certain angles, the facades seemed as iridescent as mother-of-pearl. The shutters were perfect: the tonality of the paint betrayed a supremely assured and subtle understanding of color and its interactions. There were gradations of green over exquisite pinks which the sun brought to glory in the mixture of lime and sand, blues scumbled over grayish whites and a hundred examples of that harmony of browns, light ochres, and dull purple found in Giotto. This was an aristocrat among lower-class areas. Hardly anyone was about in these huge streets: a massive woman coming back from the market, a few children playing. Unfortunately, the noise of the engine prevented me from experiencing the silence of those streets. If I had to live in Turin, I should like to live behind one of those shutters. It was a place where misanthropy was impossible.

Just where the highway began, at the top of a little hump, we saw the yellowish plain intersected by muddy channels. There were some fairly high mounds, possibly rising to fifty to sixty meters, set down quite arbitrarily in the fields, and even the hills on the other bank of the Pô reminded me of the artificial mountains which the Chinese were said to have raised in the outer suburbs of Peking. But I was in a strange land; it was better to go willingly and to play fair. I could take the risk. After all, that was why I was there. When it was a question of enjoying whatever benefits the journey might bring, I was no more afraid of scorn than the people I had met the night before on the Via Garibaldi.

It was a very fine day now, with a not-too-lively sky of the kind I like. The light was soft. Far off to our left we could see the real mountains amidst golden, effervescent mists.

How was Antoine's headache? Quite bad. Nevertheless, he was doing eighty according to the speedometer, and the road was so smooth that we glided along as if on a flying carpet. I could even have been writing if I had felt like it. I didn't want to do that, but I made some calculations on the map. That was part of the game it amused me to play, like taking the highway when I thought that roads should be provided specifically for slow driving.

All the same, I was sorry that I had asked to go by this highway, in spite of the eighty kilometers an hour and the silken surface. To our right was a yellow road that would allow us to visit Chivasso, where the princes of Monferrat minted their golden florins. Now we were driving through a jumble of vast publicity hoardings that formed a diorama on either side of us. But they did not trouble me for long, and anyway I thought they were fun at first, a pleasure that should not be underestimated. Then, just as quickly, I had totally forgotten them. I have the same ability to carry on dreaming or working while listening to, or even, according to my friends, taking part in, a conversation in which they say I make as much sense as anyone else, although my participation is automatic. All my attention is actually somewhere else entirely. This time it was on the countryside, which had markedly improved for the last twenty kilometers or so.

This, to be sure, will be sufficient for the all too fastidious and knowing to dismiss me with a shrewd smile. What, they will say, happy again and you're scarcely past Turin? I readily acknowledge that I am easily pleased. I am nearly always delighted, even by a monkey dancing to the music of a barrel organ. I am far from demanding and hate to seem over-censorious.

The sky was taking advantage of the morning to put on a sumptuous display that would not have disgraced the Sacred Congregation of Rites in Rome. But we were surely the only laity at the ceremony. The travelers we came across were tightly encased in their steel chests. The roofs of their vehicles were drawn over their eyes like the visors of helmets, or like monks' hoods. They were hundred-and-fifty-kilometers-an-hour hermits. They snapped across us as fast as a whip crack or whistled past us like rushes in the wind. All their attention was on the speedometer and the road so many yards ahead. For the most part, their passengers were wealthy women very much en route, and solemnly enclosed in the leaden heaviness of high-speed travel. What could they possibly have to offer on arrival?

The sky was certainly magnificent above the plains. Today it was pulling out all the stops. Its every aspect was gold-tinted, and it was covered with flamboyant clouds. There was a constant transition from sun to shadow. The alternating experiences of hot and cold made us all the more sensitive. The horizon supplied the background you usually expect in a vast canvas of some grandiose event such as a martyrdom, a battle, a wedding, or a canonization.

Along the edges of the fields they had planted rows of birch trees and aspens, so generously that we seemed to be passing through a forest. We felt that it must be the same for thousands and thousands of square miles roundabout. I had always seen these trees sacrificed and destroyed everywhere because their wood was not "economically viable." Their condition here indicated several hundred years of loving care. They were very tall and very slender. The overwhelming impression was one of youthfulness, for if the least wind brushed their highly sensitive leaves their mood changed instantly from high spirits to gloom. You saw them leaning over the dark waterways along which they grew, wholly conscious, I was sure, of what they were about. They were pruned up to nine or ten meters and were sometimes fifteen and even twenty meters in height. This treatment brought out all the beauty of the trunks, which were never stiff like poplars, but as lithe and captivating as the torso of a youth more than a little aware of himself, whose white skin (or, rather, as here, piebald bark) had the sheen of a well-cared-for horse's coat, and who was confident, above all, of love and affection. I am sure that they were lopped for strictly arboricultural reasons, but it was done intelligently (even, perhaps, gently, delicately), and the result was before us. The sight of those high branches into which all the strength of the sap was thus made to rise was truly reassuring. It was life in all its tenderness, divorced from crime and the need to kill. This was much more cheerful than the springtime gamboling of any lamb; here there were no reservations. This, rather than philosophers, was the source of moments of nobility. Surely the people of this area were not eaten up by a desire to emulate those miserable wretches who have reached the approved niche, and stay there, no longer aware of the happiness of being out under trees to which you have consecrated twenty years of devoted effort.

These thickets were to be found wherever Piedmont bordered on Lombardy. Whenever the road took us onto a bridge over a roadway below, we saw the forest of birches and poplars stretching out to infinity. A bell tower would emerge from afar, or flights of ducks and plover would lift up from it. Occasionally it would open onto a larger rice field in front of a farm with a chain pump, wind engine, silos, and chapel; or it would stretch along a roadway at the end of which stood the twenty-violet-windowed facade of some gentleman's residence. Behind the stripwork of its white trunks, it would hide apparently deserted white villages that came into view, and then disappeared under those micaed leaves and into the tracery of branches. I thought of peaceful roadways, of stretches of water; I glimpsed bronze-green rice fields. A black horse with a long mane was galloping for sheer enjoyment in a meadow. Above the trees, towns and villages showed towers encircled by four or five rows of embrasures, campaniles surmounted by octagonal loggias with serrated eaves, or the fullness of a heavy parish church in the Lombard style strongly redolent of banks and counting rooms. Every now and then there was a stream or a river, as the Orco, the Dora, the Elvo, or the Cervo opened out through the vast golden expanses of mixed wood- and pasturelands, where minute waterways twisted among the mud and stones. Toward the south, the horizon appeared in these gaps, as reflective as the sea. Everywhere we saw aspens and birches, brown rice fields, yellowing stone bell towers, and the pink brickwork of houses. Now the fields were more elongated and revealed groups of women trussing the rice. They wore fiercely colored skirts—red, yellow, and sometimes an even more intense if pure white. The farms had churches with the same claim to magnificence as Milan Cathedral. These were chubby edifices, got up to the nines, with exposed stonework carefully worked and trimmed in every recess, and patron saints held between the pursed lips of the mouths they opened flush, as it were, with the rice fields. They were flanked by silos, police and fire stations, warehouses, stables, barns, and garages decorated with potted geraniums.

The Alps bordered this entire region in the north. Since they were very close, thirty kilometers at most, they rose above the trees everywhere. They seemed made of black velvet. Today the rain was coming down in torrents. You could see little red clouds connected to the earth by a light tissue of gossamer threads.

Without mountains so close, and especially mountains with lakes, I could never explain the Piedmontese character. Those who dwell in wood- and pasturelands where maize and rice grow so abundantly, and who, after having eaten regularly and generously, spend their time with such ever inoffensive companions as the trees in all their silent beauty, have a marked inclination to resort to fine sentiments and to scorn action. They are well aware how they should avenge an insult to honor, or throw off oppression. Their poets tell them how, and there are four or five of them to a village. But the people think they have done enough if they recite the heroic lay by heart, and especially if they go so far as to roll their eyes, and fiercely too, at the narrator, while merely listening. As soon as the inhabitants of Casapinta de Croce di Mosso, of Cressa de Fontanetto, reach twenty, they descend to the plains. There they get married and blend their stock, just as if they were mixing wines. I was told a story that gives a good idea of how they think in the forests up above Biella and Varallo. My friend Bernardo had a house at Scopa in the high valley of the Sesia. A very spirited housekeeper had looked after him for thirty years. She had never failed to look on the bright side of things. Recently, however, this good humor had disappeared all of a sudden. Just as abruptly, Bernardo thought: "She's been cheating me!" (Though of course she had accounted for every centime throughout those thirty years.) He took down a little box he had hidden in the library, behind the three volumes of Tronchi's *Annals of Pistoia*, and in which he kept five or six gold coins. They had vanished. He said nothing and life went on as before. My friend lived on his own in the house at Scopa with this woman, who was about fifty, enormous, and with a mustache which had caused Bernardo to remark to me: "Perhaps it's a man. No one's been close enough to look!" When it was winter and wood was needed, she cut down the pines very dextrously and carried the logs on her back. Nothing was locked in that old sixteenth-century house where not even five-hundred-lire worth of repairs had been carried out over more than three centuries. There were often crimes in that mountain area, and they were always unpremeditated. Nine times out of ten, even though they were crimes committed for gain of some kind, the murderer took his or her own life afterward. Bernardo went on living with the maid, whose jovial manner quite disappeared. On some days she even displayed that absolute, definitive sadness of the eyes that makes them shine out strangely from an otherwise haggard face. This situation lasted three years (the aspect of interest to the initiated) while Bernardo finished his work on the history of Bologna. Eventually, one fine day, Ghita (the actual name of the woman, who was known as Marguerite) brought Bernardo his morning coffee, and he saw that she was smiling quite openly as she used to, and that her eyes were as lively as ever they had been. He drank his coffee without foreboding. As soon as he was up, he went to the box. There were the gold coins, as before.

I related this story in Turin. They added something which gives the whole thing an even more Piedmontese twist. "Bernardo lied at least once," they said, "and in a way very common here. We don't think he went to inspect the little box behind the *Annals of Pistoia* when Ghita became so melancholy, but trusted to Providence: *He put God on his side.*"

We crossed the Ticino when we left Piedmont. We stopped on the bridge spanning the river, which reminded me of the Durance. There was the same vast riverbed that spoke of cosmic fury long ago. But here the mud was yellow.

In Lombardy the rice fields were bigger and the trees more sparse. The little towns and villages seemed just set down without foundations in spaces which the sun invested with its misty light. These were affluent and often new agglomerations. Nothing much, except for the hill of Abbiate Grasso, stood out for the contemplative eye. You could cross without noticing it the battlefield of Magenta where, on 4 June 1859, the French and Sardinians defeated the Austrians. Before he reenlisted, my maternal grandfather (yet another), who later became first trombone player in the Imperial Guard (of

AN ITALIAN JOURNEY

Napoleon III), began his service as a Zouave in this area. He had to leap over these streams in spite of his baggy red trousers. What was my other grandfather doing at the time? No enthusiast for bayonet charges, he would polish off all his opponents under cover of darkness and certainly from behind.

We got to Milan at midday. This was Antoine's first victory. Thanks to our Italian Automobile Club sticker (bought at the frontier for a thousand lire), we were able to park the car free of charge to the right of the Duomo, on the little square before the Palazzo Reale and in a very flattering category. Now it was a question of negotiating a scorchingly hot city. We were famished, it was close, the light was blinding, and the Duomo irritating with all its spires. Antoine and Germaine took advantage of the chance to be photographed with some pigeons. At last, in a side street, we chose a restaurant with a window display of two or three kilos of pasta. This had been treated with miniature curling tongs, and looked as if it had come out of a Bruges lace-making machine. We carried on making the most of what we found, and ate a first-class beef-and-mutton stew with potatoes, carrots, leeks, turnips, and so on. Then we had to deal with Antoine's headache once again, which was getting worse and worse. Besides, he was as red as a turkey cock. He talked about taking a hotel room to lie down for a while. He was worn out. The easiest thing to do was to stay the night in Milan.

We went outside again, into the unbearable heat and light of the street. The air was thick with a blistering dust like that released by plane-tree pompoms in the spring. Even in normal weather, I heartily dislike those first hours of the afternoon, but to walk around on the pavements then was more than I could stand. I looked gloomily at the most sensitive

Italians in the peninsula. The streets may have been packed with the most unusual women, but I saw none. If I was to believe what I had read, I was among the most romantic men in the world, and yet there was only one thought in my mind: to be able to stretch out in the shaded light of a cool bedroom. We had not even the strength left to make a decision. To enter a hotel lobby and start talking to the reception clerk seemed to me beyond the realm of the possible. Antoine was overnursing his headache; Elise and Germaine were fascinated by the shop windows laden with useless things (also priced in lire with lines of zeroes) that adhered relentlessly to their longing until they had been bought, and were just as readily thrown into some quite obscure corner. Silently I told the gods that I would have been better off at home.

I scarcely know more of Milan than a single street. It was very small and like a river's minor tributary where the silent water hardly quivers. I cannot remember the name. It was a street four or five meters wide at most, bordering on the warehouses of a big store. It was on the left side of the Duomo. It must have been at right angles to the Corso Vittorio Emmanuelle. I swear that at two in the afternoon, on that day and in my then state of mind, it was the most hateful place in the whole world.

And then there was the Duomo, which wasn't worth a cuss.

Finally, we sat down on a café terrace with an excellent view of this horror. It wasn't its exuberance that annoyed me, but the fact that its sumptuousness was wholly lacking in generosity. It just wasn't accessible. A particular statue, which seemed very beautiful when I saw a photograph of it in favorable circumstances, was now a hundred meters away from me. I couldn't enjoy it any longer. It was only an outline, a shadow figure playing a part quite different from that called for by its actual beauty. Even the excessive lavishness wasn't the essential fault. To be satisfied with very little is not necessarily a sign of sound judgment, elegance, or beauty (for it often betrays a quite childish degree of self-conceit). What is wrong is useless abundance from which no one can possibly benefit.

More than eight hundred of the two thousand three hundred statues of the Duomo were carved before 1380. In southern countries Romanesque art lasted well beyond the twelfth century. I had learned from Scipione Olivari that much of the sculpture had been produced in the thirteenth, fourteenth, and fifteenth centuries by quite independent stonemasons who lived in the countryside. That did not worry them. The additional orders arrived late in those outlying areas where no one went very often who wasn't prepared to lose a horse, and where there was so little reason to think of art as a kind of sacred labor performed by priests. This was why, for example, I found so much inspiration in the figure of Job (to the left at the top of the staircase leading to the tomb of the Medici), and in an extraordinary Christ who, though bearing the cross, *was actually smiling*. Undoubtedly there is much of the Seine-et-Oise (and even of the Meuse and Rhine) in the smiling statue of Reims. It is a smile for men with long blond mustaches who can sleep easily after slaughter. All that fervent if dark land—which sometimes enjoyed the feeling of remorse even in advance—was in the smile I contemplated at Milan. Scipione, indeed, had shown me a whole series of quasi-columnar statues in which life hung by a thread; that is, which could captivate and subdue even the most stoutly principled of self-opinionated onlookers. Then there were those arched bays where playing-card kings hunted stags through the interwoven trees of stone forests. Against the whole background of Lombardy and the Alps, you had only to gaze at the wall there, and peer into the uttermost recesses of that variegated scene, to find the life of the very same country expressed without the least exaggeration before your everyday eyes. The outer limits of discretion, to be sure, were often reached, as in the capital showing suicides crowned with roses, or in that where the thieves had become not robbers but murderers.

What pride lies concealed in Romanesque humility! Seen thus, the Duomo is a modest monument.

Now Germaine, Elise, and Antoine wanted to stay where they were. They were fixed in their comfortable chairs and the whole restaurant (all possible delights, indeed) seemed at their disposal. I hailed a taxi and went to see Ivo Senesi, who was waiting for me. The Milan I observed on the way to the Via Beato Angelico was like any southern (though not too southern) city in strong sunlight. I talked about art with Senesi and his wife. I had never met them before; they were very interesting. Their flat was on the sixth floor of a suburban house from which we could see the roofs of the city generously marked by the spreading leaves of the treetops emerging from big parks and gardens. Five minutes after introductions we were discussing Dante. I took the same taxi back to the Piazza del Duomo. The driver had waited for me outside, free of charge. I found my three children duly relaxed. How was Antoine's headache? All right. So right that we decided to take to the road again.

It was five o'clock and cooler now. Above all, the light was soft. As at Turin, we went round the town, where we rediscovered the bronze statue of the mounted Academician at every crossroads. He was striking very heroic poses, including the one in which he had come a cropper. Perhaps, after all, it was not meant to be so humorous.

We rolled past cheerless hills. Evening was falling as we approached Bergamo. One of my neighbors at Manosque came from there. He cared for his vegetable garden just under my study window. I often watched him at work: using his big rake to get the spinach beds ready, sowing his potatoes and haricot beans, or breaking up the ground with his three-pronged fork. There was no doubt: this was precisely the area he could have come from. I pointed out the neatness of the little gardens to Elise. It was from here that old Negroni had brought the cast of mind that made him plant flowers alongside his vegetables, and surely his generous nature and the equable temperament that made him ready to take three francs for what would have cost thirty in town. Of course he thought of Fine as a fellow countrywoman (although she was from the Piedmontese Alps).

I knew someone else from Bergamo. This was so much the case that his friends gave him the surname Bergues, and no one knew his real name any longer. Gide said to me: "I find that man obnoxious." This was significant, for Gide rarely detested anyone. He would play chess with me in the back room of a mountain bar. I maintained a firm friendship with Bergues. This unusual man was the virtual *condottiere* of a national forest covering several thousand hectares. After a long period as an official woodcutter, he had become—no less officially—a finder of medicinal plants. He collected scabious, vanilla orchid roots, datura, and artemisia; and also mushrooms, raspberries, strawberries, and blueberries. But he caught trout by hand without taking the least notice of official prohibitions, and set traps for foxes, hares, marmots, and badgers. He was very skilled at tanning hides, and his house reeked fearsomely. When he saw us playing chess, he would come over and sit down by us. I think he was especially fond of Gide, and particularly liked his style at chess. On such occasions Gide was a veritable Castruccio Castraccani, and as ambitious in the game as that medieval Ghibelline soldier of fortune who became Duke of Lucca was politically. You could see that from his face. Yet Bergues did not lose an atom of a move. But there was another reason why Gide disliked him so (though perhaps he detested him on account of chess too). Bergues did not utter a word. On the table, next to the chessboard, he would set down three or four frogs which the cold marble kept immobile. From time to time he would swallow one of them alive and whole, helping it down with a generous glass of wine, and never saying anything. Once he had finished the frogs, he would leave. That was a great help to me sometimes, when I risked being checkmated. Essentially, these were sessions, even lessons, in Italianism.

The lower city of Bergamo emerged from a small marshy plain brown with rushes. The town itself, set up on its hill, with Santa Maria Maggiore, its Duomo, its Rocca, and San Michele al Pozzo Bianco, black trees and silence, was a frog-swallower. I can't put it any other way. It reminded me of Shakespeare's Juliet: "What man art thou, that, thus bescreen'd in night, / So stumblest on my counsel?" This was the perfect place for my Angelo Pardi, the Piedmontese colonel of hussars in *The Horseman on the Roof*. The Duchess of Ezzia was too sensitive for me to let her moulder in a cupboard in Turin. It was clear to me what Angelo might have done with a town like this. The night was not yet dark enough to suppress the pink tiles that were replacing the rushes. The wind could easily deal with these marshes. For seven years I had been wondering where Carlotta came from. She had the same nature as Bergues. Just think of that young woman in a forest of Austrian soldiers! Novels do not say everything. I had often puzzled over the right way to convey what they have to leave out. Cars, trains, any vehicles that allow the countryside to pass before your eyes at an unwonted speed are spurs to the imagination. Walking is a matter of style, but speed prompts action. Before entering that little world stricken by cholera, Angelo had lived intensely. You could see that from his memories. He had stayed at Aix-en-Provence for a fairly long time. There he even met a certain Anna Clève, who was an opera singer and with whom he had an affair. And it was his own fault if that did not work out. He became involved in the affairs of a vicar-general. But there is not a word about all this in my novel. After having survived the cholera episode, and having (as he thought) left Pauline de Théus for good, he returned to Italy. But the Italian war of independence was still in the future. We would probably see him again in the course of the celebrated Cigar Day in Milan. The Milanese stopped smoking to protest the Austrian emperor's response to their claims. The police distributed cigars to soldiers and even to prisoners, hoping to provoke a reaction that would entitle them to use force. Maddeningly cigar-in-mouth soldiers and policemen paraded in the streets. In short, there were five deaths and many wounded. Thereafter the Milanese stopped walking on the Corso, where these "massacres" (as the popular tracts put it) took place. This did not mean that they ceased strolling altogether. Instead they took to the approach to the Porta Romana. Angelo, whom we had seen smoking so many little cigars, could not have ignored a day like this. At least, I do not think he would have. But a year and a half, perhaps two years, or twenty months, let us say, must have passed between the point at which he returned to Italy on the horse bought from Théus and the moment when the rebellion broke out. What did he do in the interval? There was Giuseppe, and Lavinia; there was his mother, then Carlotta, and Signor Stratigopolo, of course. There were those brown marshes, these pink tiles, and the town up there; and Piedmont and Lombardy. There were even my friends Bernardo, Sciopone, Ivo Senesi, Bergues, Negroni, and Gide playing chess. I should like (I thought) to write about what happens when fictive people encounter and are embellished by real people. A source of lively narrative indeed. But I was forgetting: there was my grandfather too. Not the Zouave—the other one.

After Bergamo we came across a tower. Although it was the exact likeness of one of those watchtowers—jealous guardians indeed—that the grim seigneurs of the Middle Ages erected in the thickly wooded countryside, it was undeniably modern. It seemed to have been stuck in the corner of an abandoned airfield (still covered with brown rushes and reeds). Two electricians were rolling wire onto a drum at the foot of a telegraph pole. I asked them what the monument was. They stared at it as if they had never seen it before (or had always seen it there). They didn't know. One of them said: "Mussolini perhaps." A very big tower to end up as a miserable "perhaps."

The women with the most beautiful eyes in Italy were said to come from Brescia. We were well into the night when we turned off into the road leading to it. For me, the headlights, which made greens seem so uncannily intense, revealed a roadway bordered with poplars and meadows like one of the Alpine roads I liked so much. But then I was ready to find anything beautiful. For example, I noticed one stately arch that served as a mundane railway bridge.

But the streets we were negotiating now were very badly

lit by sparse lamps and absolutely deserted (it was only eight in the evening). They led us between bare walls five to six meters high, like those of barracks, prisons, or fortresses. I did not always find this military preference distasteful; on the contrary. We were moving about in an operatic setting during the very scene when the tyrant executes his evil designs. We wove our way through these fortified embankments without meeting a living soul. Clearly, we were driving around in a circle. Antoine was enchanted. He accepted an invitation if any opening proffered one, turning right, then left, right again, back again: whirling, circling, twirling. We passed that high ironbound gate at least three times. "What a very odd town!" said Germaine. "What's it called?" asked Elise. I replied, "Brescia, so it says."

Eventually, for reasons unknown, we entered a side street and emerged in a square where our experience of unreality reached its culminating moment. Suddenly we stopped. As before, there was absolutely no living person to be seen. Under lights so intensely white that they sent a shiver down our backs, we were confronted by the cut-out stage set of a turn-of-the-century Russian house such as you might find in Turgenev's *A Sportsman's Sketches*. On the courtyard side you could see, though obliquely, the pediment and balcony of a little rococo palace with steps leading up to it. On the garden side you were faced by a straightforward brick-built house; its interior was visible on the ground floor through a wide and suitably theatrical bay windowed entrance, behind which you spied the metal labels of bottles on shelves. "Shit!" said Antoine (who is usually quite polite), and apologized immediately. All four of us agreed with him entirely.

Silence reigned. "This isn't Brescia," Antoine remarked. "It just isn't possible! I don't know what it is. It's bittersweet. It's a dream. On the garden side it's probably a café." He went to try the door. The bell rang and eventually an actor appeared. An actor, indeed. We were both disappointed and fascinated. He spoke and even made gestures. He indicated an empty street that rose before us under the yellow lamplight.

I had never seen anything more romantic than the outer avenues of Brescia at night. Leaving this eloquent setting, we returned to the somewhat threadbare darkness of the first act. Gone were the fortress and the embankments, but on either side of us stretched a black expanse of gardens, trees, and thickets which our headlights daubed with green spinach at the bends. We were entering a long, wide, and unbelievably circumspect avenue.

We checked our wristwatches. Yes, it was half past eight. "How many inhabitants did you say?" Antoine asked me. I looked in the guidebook: "A hundred and forty-seven thousand!" We had spied one of them anyway: the actor from the stage restaurant. We had been roaming about this town or, more precisely, had been lost in a labyrinthine conundrum, for almost half an hour.

Now we were proceeding at a quite discreet speed along a very broad park avenue. To left and right we could hardly make out the white of the facades with their shutters and doors closed. You would have thought that the streetlamps had nothing to do with civilization, and that they were lights as natural as the stars and glowworms. Anyway, they revealed no more than such natural sources would. We were in a kind of artificial looking-glass world. Using real trees, real leaves, and real houses, they had managed (I am sure that it was the effect of the light: of the blinding effects a while before and of the present gloom) to give the impression of painted cardboard stage sets. All the volumes had been flattened. The lack of characters completed the illusion. We were no longer convinced that even we ourselves were at all substantial.

It seemed that we ought to take the first turn to the left. But were there any turns? Was that the way into a street or merely a brown outline on a stage flat? I had never seen Antoine drive so carefully. Nevertheless, we pointed the front end leftward and gingerly started to penetrate what otherwise we would have called a street.

It was very narrow. And it was long and dark. Within a few seconds we were crossing another long, dark street. Still no one around. To right and left we could discern walls, interrupted here and there by vast closed doors. At last a shadow crossed before us and stopped to let us pass. There, as I went by, I saw the second inhabitant of Brescia, squeezed into a corner.

After that, we suddenly came across four others at a crossing. They were in front of a piece of scenery masquerading as a tobacconist's. The suits they wore were up-to-date, but one of them, in his workman's overalls, stood out from the others. They looked as if they were rehearsing or even acting out a scene that surely had to do with heroism in some, certainly very noble, way. The poses they struck were very fine.

Very slowly, we were approaching the center of the drama. The street broadened out, and we were once more under the strong white light of act 2 before we entered what was undoubtedly the main setting.

In spite of our near-walking speed, Antoine put the brake on firmly. We were entering a new stage set, a large square that was both sixteenth and twentieth century and entirely new. In front of us, illuminated from top to bottom, was a vast square tower. Or a fourteen-story skyscraper, supported by arcades and carrying even more arcades into the remoteness of a blue night above, itself imitated to perfection, with every star in place. All around the square in the bright cold light ran a series of porticoed spaces where the men and women extras (surely) of the opera were strolling. Quite new cars, golden cars it seemed, were parked in front of a little peristyle. There were a hundred or so people in the square itself. Composed, immobile, or betraying life only by walking so very slowly, they were clearly awaiting the movement of the conductor's baton. There was not a sound beyond the whispering you would expect before a performance. You could hear coughs from the orchestra stalls.

I was sure that we had arrived late and that the last bells would soon ring. Perhaps it was our fault that the show hadn't started. What a nerve to enter the theater and even appear onstage in a car! I wished I was down a rabbit hole.

Something just had to be done, so we stupidly asked one of the extras moving along the pavement close to us if there was a hotel nearby. You ask such ridiculous questions only in dreams. The answer you get is what you would expect in a dream. The impassive character pointed to the street opposite.

We made our way there, taking care to match our pace to that of the setting. I had the comforting feeling that we scarcely bothered them. Our entrance may have been star-tling, but our exit was a matter of general indifference.

The street we had been directed to was pleasant. It was divided lengthwise by a vaulted gallery which raised the height by about a meter and had two or three steps leading up to it every now and then. The part we were driving along was still bathed in that unreal white light. The effect was something like that of an extra-intense full moon. The vaulted part was softly shadowed and dotted with little yellow lamps.

You would have thought it inhabited by great lazy fishes, like an aquarium at night.

We were reassured as soon as we went into the hotel. Here we were at last in a familiar setting; it was that of act 2, scene 2, of Laurence Olivier's *Hamlet:* "A room in the castle." The rooms they offered us were supposed to be "for married couples." That is to say, they each held two bachelor beds with five meters between them. The price they asked seemed outrageous even in lire. We thanked Polonius and departed to find somewhere else.

Finally, a few yards away, we found a place. The building had been damaged by English bombers in World War II. They had not quite finished putting it to rights. There was still scaffolding inside, here and there. But all this was refreshingly earthly. I would not surrender this too, too solid ground. Here I would stay. Elise and I chose the only habitable room on the second floor. Antoine and Germaine were on the first, which had been restored to full modern comfort. My window looked out on an old Jesuit-style monastery façade, the old tiles of real rooftops for some distance, and a belfry that actually served as a belfry and sounded the hour quite normally. This I found truly satisfactory.

But now we had to go out to eat. We strolled along the empty streets. To be alone with a town is an attractive proposition. You can imbue houses with the feelings that you would usually ascribe to passersby. The main characteristic here was a kind of folk heroism. It was like reviewing an assembly of veterans of Napoleon's Old Guard. Then there was the silence, with conspiratorial whispers from the colonnades, and that lighting: I had never seen anything like before, except in a theater.

When you arrive in any city at night, to be sure, it can easily seem mysterious. This was the same, but in a different way. The street where we looked for somewhere to eat, for instance, stretched out like any normal big street with shops and even a lawyer's nameplate, but finished up as a dark, narrow byway from which a trolleybus emerged, all but scraping the walls. The bus was decorated with flickering red and green lights and was quite empty: it was like an ambulating pickle jar. We retraced our steps. It was half past nine and we were hungry. We went up another street and it threatened to become a tunnel.

At last we found a trattoria where they made us some marvelous meat dishes and pasta. The wine was superb. Two cyclists came in, put their machines against the wall, sat down next to us, and immediately started playing rummy.

We finished the evening underneath the arcades, on the terraces of a little café. These impetuously imaginative people had been wise enough to produce a duly civilized version of one of the oldest delights this world affords: sitting down at your ease with other people in the cool of the evening. The Italians are said to be noisy and to gesticulate, but that is a libel dreamed up by the English. In my opinion, no one above an imaginary line from Briançon to La Rochelle has any idea of what a restaurant terrace should be like. Some in Paris and in Stockholm are acceptable, but they really know how to get the best out of them in Italy. Even in Marseilles they have no conception. I spent more than two hours in Brescia admiring the abilities of the people around us. There were many pretty women, and men bold enough to show themselves as very devils when seated. It was not a smart or fashionable café (this was no Parisian Deux-Magots). There were local shopkeepers, the man from the garage, the electrician, the clockmaker, the hosier. They kept their voices down when they did talk, without making a single gesture, after long intervals of silence. The men smoked those acrid little cigars after which even a glass of cold water is like a gift from heaven. They did not talk business. Instead I heard some very lyrical phraseology. I had rediscovered the charm of Turin. Here it was simply a matter of being happy and of reaching that state by very skilled procedures. To do that, of course, you needed the spirit of enthusiasm, well versed and well exercised. No one was bored for a single minute that evening. Yet there was no sight to see. All this went on under the arcades of the Corso Zanardelli, which is exactly a hundred meters long and scarcely fifteen wide. The word *corso* can be misleading. I discovered later that it was merely the former center of the old Renaissance Brescia, contained then between the present Via dei Patrioti, Via dei Mille, Via Pusterla, and the Castello hill. It was and remains a *corso* reserved to its particular use, a little *corso* in a fortified town. It was hardly two meters from there to the ramparts (on the site of which the Via dei Patrioti runs), yet that space contained the old rooftops, the bell tower, and the Jesuit church I could see from my hotel window. Accordingly it was an area that would have been exposed "to enemy fire" if it had been too open. There was no hint of the elevated gentility of the Turin arcades on the terraces of the two adjoining cafés where we spent that evening, and where so much intimate knowledge of the art of living was revealed. The arcades of Brescia were low and squat, like the vaults you came across in mountain stables. In their shelter you could soon acquire a form of serenity much akin to that of a field mouse just pointing its nose at the edge of a hole. An aptitude like that was essential in an imaginative region, for it entitled you to avoid currying favor with anyone. This attitude (which covered everything, including political influence) did not bother with love (or was a long way from what is usually understood by that euphemism). Even though seven or eight very good looking women were present, I never noticed anyone looking with an eye to the main chance or heard a single honeyed word. All the men seemed very intent on cherishing their little cigars, the very reek of which was enough to inhibit the designs of a would-be Lothario. There were little boxes of them on the tables, and I saw women (far from ugly too) asking for a few puffs of a cigar that was already going. This was generally accepted. I am sure that there was nothing unacceptable on that café terrace. It was a spot absolutely devoid of vanity.

III

Brescia, Peschiera, Verona

I wasn't wrong about the clock. I stayed awake to savor the silence of Brescia, and counted the harmonious sounds one by one as the hour struck. There was a light wind that night, and I could hear it whistling its way to us over the hills.

I got up very early, leaving Elise asleep, and went into the town on my own. At six o'clock in the morning the faint straw-yellow sunlight fell obliquely on the Corso Zanardelli, reaching all the way into the gallery beneath the arcades.

An attractive young woman operated the coffee machine, a very handsome device, in the café where we had spent the evening before on the terrace. She told me that the baker had not yet delivered the croissants: the Signor Cavaliere would have to wait a little while. I felt very honored by the title she gave me.

I had noticed another young woman standing behind a bank of cakes and pastries. She now came out to join us, and the two of them flirted with me mildly while I waited for the rolls. I congratulated them on their magnificent percolator, and they promptly set it in motion for me. This produced such a medley of whistling, seething, and variegated jets of steam that we all feared an explosion. The waiter scattering sawdust about the place came over and reestablished order; or, rather, elicited the deeper meaning of the existing disorder for me. He explained that the apparatus was not really supposed to release gusts of steam; when operated proficiently it could supply seven to eight different types of coffee. He gave me to understand that he was the expert in this particular field. Thereupon, the girls decided to test his expertise and asked me to judge the outcome. The waiter was put on the spot but seemed to welcome the challenge. Four empty coffee cups were ranged on the counter for these four inspectors now engaged in a highly serious monitoring procedure. After a single and, I thought, very adroit manipulation of the mechanism, the cups were filled to the brim. The waiter asked me what I thought of the coffee. "Superb!" (of course). He turned to the girls in triumph. They confirmed its excellence. This was hardly surprising, for everyone knew that this was where you got the best coffee in Brescia. Nevertheless, we had to watch him carry out a second manipulation which, I must admit, left me rather baffled. He had simultaneously to remove a cover, press a bar, turn a wheel, close a tap, and strike a specific lever very fiercely with his fist. The machine bucked like a rodeo horse. The young women stepped back. The waiter reassured them with an infinitely understanding smile and, in the tones of a general fresh from a famous victory, told them to move the cups closer. Once again, they were filled to the brim. "Superb!" But *No! No!* and again *No!:* they pointed out an all but imperceptible brownish residue inside the cup. This evoked a lively discussion packed with technical terminology. I was forced to play the dumb witness, and the girls looked utterly vanquished. The waiter, however, affected the nicely judged degree of modest triumph that losers always find most galling. A customer in a long brown raincoat came in. He too had to say what he thought. His technical vocabulary was equal if not superior to that of the three specialists.

He discovered the traces of certain precious etheric oils in the slight residue. These, he maintained, accounted for the coffee's exceptional flavor. He emphasized his point for everyone in general, and for me in particular, by repeatedly clacking his tongue against his palate. His whole behavior was designed to stress his hope that we had realized the supreme importance of this somewhat recherché point. It was a great moment. As we contemplated it appropriately, the man in the raincoat profited from the delay and pulled a three-month-old puppy right out of his chest, so to speak. The two women appeared never to have seen its like. I was very taken by the eyes of the girl who had first operated the machine: they were suddenly alive with all the fire of passionate intensity. She cooed; she warbled; she emitted tender little cries that made me as embarrassed as I would have been to hear them in a somewhat different situation. But here there was no such thing as reserve or discretion. No one was reluctant to be caught in a moment of passionate near-ecstasy. To protect the little creature's paws from the cold zinc counter, they interposed a card-player's mat between flesh and metal. The first girl rubbed the little dog against her face. It was a spaniel puppy, with a bluish tinge. It would always look like that, I thought. It would be sad for the rest of its life. By now they had called on nearly all the devices of tender affection. Everyone, even two or three customers who had entered after the event, seemed anxious to exhaust the vocabulary of endearment.

The baker arrived with his croissants. In the meantime, they had told me a whole Arthurian cycle of stories about the tiny creature's mother and father. Finally, they discussed its future as if it were that of some young prince or princess. Then they drank their cappuccinos and ate their croissants with sage contentment.

Surely I do not have to insist that I had made this trip not to get to know Italy but to be happy. And now I was happy. I was quite at ease with these people. They never put on airs like those Italians who imagined they were captains of the Papal Guard, so to speak; or those who played at being cold, haughty English men and women. Vanity makes me feel uneasy. I don't find it amusing. I have seen how it can lead imperceptibly to crime and how it can degrade its practitioners. Even in its least offensive form, vanity makes people inclined to betray friendship. I never know what to say to a conceited person. I tend to clam up in their presence instead of making an easy retort. I just surrender to the situation and either say nothing at all or walk out immediately, which means that the chance of happiness always disappears too. When I was younger I was prepared to waste time on people like that. Now I prefer to expend my patience on better things. This does not mean that I have turned sour. Not in the least. When I am with a group of people like those in the little café in Brescia that day, I find that capacity for spontaneous, almost totally uninhibited enjoyment, with absolutely no reference to any kind of deity, irresistibly infectious. The men and women who had played with the nickel-plated coffee machine and with the puppy were certainly not without deadly passions. Yet they helped me to see that I could be subject to similar emotions without losing my self-esteem; and that is never possible with vanity, even when it is seemingly most innocuous.

At the hairdresser's I went to after that, all the talk was of a political assassination currently before the court in Vincenza. An illustrated weekly had published photographs of various witnesses. The man in the barber's chair next to me was interested in the case. He was, it seemed, a peasant from that area and in Brescia for the market. He was looking through the magazines while having his hair cut. "I wouldn't want to owe people like that a favor," he said of the photographs. The hairdresser warned him to be more careful about what he said, and clicked his scissors admonishingly near the customer's ears. Since I was a foreigner, the peasant looked directly at me, so suspiciously that I thought it best to come out with a very long sentence in French. Although my head was right back on the rest, I tried to snatch a look at the photograph in question while the barber shaved my chin. It was a portrait of a man full of wily hatred. His features seemed to show every possible sign of complete degeneracy. Everyone appeared passionately interested in the Vincenza trial because so-called patriots were involved in it, and the acts under judgment were atrocities of a wholly unpatriotic kind.

The Via Mazzini branched off from the Corso Zanardelli, then ascended toward a tunnel that passed under the castle hill. Around 1832 my grandfather thought of Mazzini as a virtual god, capable of making the weather shine or shower. During his two years in exile from Piedmont, Mazzini had stayed in touch with all the Carbonari, who were leading an almost totally unrestrained way of life. In the nicest possible way, Jean-Baptiste Giono cut the throats of a few people in the Pinerolo area in honor of the banished Mazzini, and in obedience to some kind of contingency plan. On this occasion, however, he was not sentenced to death in absentia. The measures taken against the Sardinian government were protected by the complicity of the people as a whole, who thought of honor as something that applied only on the far bank of a river of blood. Anyway, the victims were all tools of the police in one way or another. At any rate, this was what my grandfather suggested (but did not say outright) in the little black notebook in which he recorded his revolutionary activities.

When you left the Via Mazzini and turned left into the Via Carlo Cattaneo, you came to the Palazzo Broletto, the Torre del Popolo, and the Loggia delle Gride. The Palazzo's rear facade, the one looking onto a narrow street not designed for ceremonies, prompted some of those melancholy thoughts whose absence can spoil the perfection of a bright and beautiful morning. I entered the courtyard of the Palazzo, where I felt happy for more than twenty minutes: as happy as I had been the other evening in Turin, and for no special reason. This was a place where you "caught" happiness as other people caught the plague. There was nothing out of the ordinary there, to look at anyway. It was merely the courtyard of a medieval palace with a few modern workmen on their way to the factory and some housewives heading for the market.

I strolled about the totally deserted Piazza Duomo. The Duomo Vecchio was a very beautiful Romanesque building. Like the political architecture of the Renaissance (palaces and balconies designed for conversations and executions alike), the military architecture of the Middle Ages (citadels, castles, and bastions lost in the forests) moves me, that is, gives me more vivid pleasure than the religious architecture of the tenth, eleventh, and twelfth centuries. Of course, I am as capable as anyone else of understanding the beauty of a Romanesque arch. But that kind of art appeals to me less. Above all, I neither believe that it is the sum of all beauty nor that it is an appropriate way of expressing all that needs to be expressed in art. I am not denying the particular majesty of art of this kind, but I am sure that it is best appreciated all at once, in a single flash, as it were—all too easily, I suspect. I saw Rastelli juggling around 1930, and talked to him several times in the corridors of the Cirque d'Hiver (or the Medrano—I can't quite remember which). People who knew him as well as I did agreed that he was the greatest juggler in the world. "With this art," he said laughing, "every second counts." He practiced with little phosphorescent balls until he could control them with astonishing exactitude. The paths which these balls described as they passed from one hand to the other were indeed perfect Romanesque arches. And the art of the Romanesque period also demanded a precision in which every single second counted toward the perfection of the whole. But I have time, and of all the time I have I find the time I lose most enjoyable. For me, details, everyday facts and events, even mistakes, are wonderfully diverting and teach me things that I treasure deeply. I'm quite capable of meditating in the desert. Whenever I was in prison, I found being there strangely pleasurable. I understand how people long to spend their lives shut up in monasteries, but I also like life when it has to be lived through with all its many difficulties. I have tried hard to describe the world not as it "really" is, but as it is when I add to myself to it—which, of course, does not make it any less complicated. But I have done all this, I am sure, with the necessary care. I compare and contrast my discoveries. I do not juggle with them.

Those were my thoughts during a very early morning walk in front of Brescia's two Duomos, the old and the new. The new (which dates from 1604) was not very beautiful. But, such as it was, I found it attractive in my fresh morning mood. I strolled here and there for half an hour, forgetting that I was a foreigner. I imagined that I lived in Brescia and was just taking the air before starting work. I thought of my library and my desk on the second floor of a fine house through the windows of which the gentle sunlight had just begun to pour. Then I noticed a waitress behind the curtains of a little café. She was watching me intently. "Are you waiting for anyone?" she asked. "What are you looking for?"

There were two delightful fountains on the square. One of them was called "Brescia Guerriera." Of course, I had learned an immense amount about Brescia's warlike spirit from General Govone. I had forgotten that. But now I was suddenly faced with that very spirit in bronze (or in marble or zinc). It was a kind of helmeted Pallas Athena, and very voluptuous too, being unusually well-endowed. It reminded me of Tiresias, the Theban seer blinded for watching Athena bathing. His daughter had founded a famous town fifty kilometers to the south of here.

The whole quarter near the Castello had something very gentle and unusually human about it. Carpenters planed wood, shoemakers sang, and locksmiths filed their iron so melodiously that I thought I heard willow tits in the little workshops there. Housewives chattered on their doorsteps, and one of them was sweeping the brick-paved street. A little garden of box trees grew around the statue of a young peasant soldier wearing a broad felt hat of the kind my grandfather favored. I sat down on a little bench near the fountain, and people began fetching water in order to inspect me more closely. Within a few minutes this little world was enacting a minor comedy for me. I realized that the words of praise that the workmen called out so distinctly to the women were intended to show me that nowhere in the world was so peaceful and happy as this spot. Unlike the people of northern nations, when Italians are happy they are aware of it, and want to make others happy too. Accordingly, they exaggerate

AN ITALIAN JOURNEY

things in a way that must seem inexplicable to refined people trained from early childhood to assess all the pros and cons meticulously. This tendency to extravagant overemphasis was responsible for the bold tilt to the rim of the peasant hero's hat. It also meant that he too had assuaged his egotistical passion in the grand struggle for freedom.

This area contained four or five marble plaques inserted in the walls at eye level. They bore tender inscriptions to Pyramus and Thisbe. How happy the people of this quarter must be: happy in the sense of all the centuries of true romance, as so many inscriptions and monuments celebrating their feats of arms confirmed. They were equivalent to the design of a modern engineer showing the river in terms of the bridge that one day will cross it; and the alpine valley, not for the pleasure of the meadow flowering there, but for the sake of the dam that will flood it. People have always needed a host of fairy tales in impoverished eras. The most attractive of these inscriptions was in a little alley running up to the Castello. This alleyway was unusually charming: a genuine country path in the middle of the town. Ivy, moss, and bloodwort covered garden walls behind which grew lacquer, lime, and yew trees. The path was paved with bricks in a daisy pattern. On the left-hand side as you went up there was a series of middle-class houses erected on the ramparts of a former bastion. They had polished oak doors and very pretty windows. Someone was playing a piano: not dry exercises but passages with a brilliant flourish. I can't resist translating the inscription:

"On the first of April in the year 1849, in this corpse-laden street where desperation ruled, Father Maurizio Malverti exchanged gentle words of conciliation with a vengeful enemy whose cruel souls he hoped to quell."

I have not added a single adjective here.

This quarter contained other lapidary inscriptions:

"In the years 1565 and 1869 the citizens of this town expelled their ferocious enemies from this smoking and tumultuous square."

"On this spot, on 21 March 1849 the heroic people vanquished . . . "; and so on.

I had reached the Castello. From here you could see what Brescia had been in the past, and what it was now. It had been a somewhat meager city tightly enclosed within its ramparts. I imagined it with ten to twelve thousand inhabitants: an ideal number. Now, however, it had a hundred and fifty thousand people living in innumerable pallid houses. Although the morning light was always exquisite there, and particularly so that day, it was quite unable to turn the unending sea of roofs extending beyond the Via Fratelli Ugeni, the Via N. Tartaglia, and the Via L. Da Vinci into anything approaching a pleasurable vista. This was tedium pure and simple. It was Villeurbanne, that dreary industrial suburb of Lyons, under an overwhelming thundercloud. I found this immense ensemble of mediocrity so depressing that I wanted to burn the whole thing down. The entire prospect had the ghastly uniformity of a brick warehouse in a brickworks. Looking northeast and north from the castle mound, however, I saw perfectly shaped hills inhabited by people well versed in the science of laying out gardens.

Those sunlit slopes were covered with skilfully erected dry-stone terraces. Some pines had been left there, and their dark green superbly matched the ochre earth and the silver-gray olive trees. On bare mountains farther to the east, toward Rezzato, I was sure I could see dark violet-red expanses of box that reminded me of the mountain of Lure. It had the same, almost animal shape, and the same color; it was even silhouetted against the sky in the same way. In the south, toward Mantua, the sun teased out layers of mist above somnolent marshlands.

On the way to fetch Elise from the hotel, I walked across the Piazza della Loggia with its lovely encircling porticoes. I was still in the old Brescia. Once I had looked out over those unutterable expanses of tiled roofs, I never wanted to leave this area again. Hidden under the arcades of the Corso Zanardelli, directly opposite my favorite café, we found the main theater, recognizable as such only by a few well-trodden steps and a monastery door. The whole mixture was highly reminiscent of Casanova. Moreover, the interior was Venetian, and its square-fronted boxes made it look like the façade of a prefecture. The ceiling was painted with skies, fleecy clouds, thunderclouds, and allegorical figures. It was, or rather had been, a theater famous throughout Lombardy. Towns with theaters are always resourceful. It was there that they told me the story of Giuseppe Bottari: a tale of love and retribution, but also one of love for the people.

He was a disciple of Gioberti's who left Genoa in midwinter 1847. He was making for Reggio d'Emilia, where things were stirring. Patrols from the town watch blocked the road just before Cremona, forcing him to turn off to the north. While trying to strike eastward he lost his way in the Mincio marshes. He was bringing forbidden books to sell in Italy: *Il primato morale e civile degli Italiani* (The moral and civil primacy of the Italians) by Gioberti; the *Memoirs* of General Pepe; Colletta's *History*; d'Azeglio's *Degli ultimi casi di Romagna* (The last houses of Romagna); and *Le Speranze d'Italia* (The hope of Italy) by Balbo. They were in great demand, so that he was able to hide for some time in the reed huts around

Volta. He read to the peasants, who were all sick with the fever and kept asking him to accept the rank of a general and lead them into battle. But he thought: "Ah, so they want to sell me. If they make me a general they can get a really high price for me." He decided to evade them. He had observed his most fervent and youngest disciples' ability to slip away on secret tracks through the marshes to Goito, where there was a police garrison. He hastened to Brescia, where he knew no one. He managed to get there in two days without eating. He arrived there at about ten one night, quite spent, and shivering from malaria, but carrying his books in a black bag. At the theater they were staging an opera that had done very well in Naples. The music was said to be very controversial. People had come from as far away as Milan just to take sides about this. The deserted Corso Zanardelli and the shade of its arcades tempted Bottari into resting without looking to his safety. He sat down on the worn steps that I have already mentioned. "That's right," they told me, "that's where he sat: on the steps partly occupied now by the stall of the woman who sells the French weeklies." The music he heard coming from the theater was not at all bad. They had reached the third act and they were singing a cheerful cavatina. Bottari succumbed to fatigue and to the pleasure of the music. He was found in this exhausted condition when the theatergoers streamed out. His recent exploits had made him look interestingly thin. He had feverish eyes and beautiful black hair curling over his forehead. (Later on, more than a hundred kilos of these fine locks were sold to young girls and even to romantic women.) The state he was in naturally aroused general pity, above all among the people who had just been to the opera. He evoked the special sympathy of one young woman who spoke to him kindly. She noticed his chattering teeth; when

50   AN ITALIAN JOURNEY

she touched his hand, it was almost unbearably hot. The immediate result was obvious, but the eventual outcome different from what might have been expected. Without drawing too much attention to herself, she said in a low voice: "Follow me and wait for me in front of my house." Bottari obeyed with all the speed he could muster. At last the door opened. She let him in and sat him down at a kitchen table where she had laid out a galantine of pork and some wine. There was no flirting: only tenderness and concern, with all due reticence. Bottari was twenty-six. His benefactress gave him bran water as a nostrum for the fever, and after a few minutes they began to talk a little. He was careful to make no noise; and, after cutting some bread, he was especially concerned to lay the big kitchen knife quietly on the table. "There is no need for that," said the young woman. "I am alone here for four days: my husband is away in Padua. If you like, I can even let you stay in a little room here, although I am afraid it may be too humble for you. I can see that you are a civilized person who has suffered great misfortune." This banal remark was somehow characteristic of a small provincial town and of the proximity of the black mountains reflected in a lake. Bottari, who had never killed anyone in his life, was rather confused and mentioned the forbidden books that he had with him. He gesticulated very attractively as he expounded his ideas about the importance of loving the people. If you are astonished at his naïveté, you must not forget how long he had been in the marshes among those goitrous traitors. This Scottish hospitality was reassuring, and numbed his wariness. He scrutinized the young woman. She *did not exaggerate*. She was obviously natural and sincere. He said: "Unfortunately these sensitive creatures do not really want us as their saviors." Scarcely half an hour had passed since he had entered the house. Suddenly they heard a noise outside, so loud that the echo filled the streets. Just as Bottari was gratefully swallowing (with a great deal of saliva) his first mouthful of pork, two policemen from Goito arrived in the Corso Zanardelli. They were in a very excitable state because they had galloped alone through an area thick with highly suspicious shadows. On leaving the marshes, they suddenly entered a well-lit town where people were talking under the arcades even though it was a cold winter night. The policemen were very angry, above all because they were afraid. They were also rather self-important. After all, they were bearing urgent orders regarding a revolutionary general. Some people laughed. There was a lively exchange of words. They were pushed around, so they drew their sabers. Someone fired a pistol—lo and behold! one of the gendarmes fell down dead! The other struck out around him to right and to left, and then ran in the direction of the barracks. By three o'clock they were forced to fire a small cannon to rescue the squad of soldiers that had tried to march up the Corso. At eight in the morning the dragoons from Bergamo charged the barricade at the church of San Francesco and took it by storm. It was the last to fall. They captured five or six of the people who had thrown it up, including Bottari, for he had been digging fervently with his delicate hands. They did not shoot him on the spot but kept him in a cell for eight days. Many passionate words were uttered on his behalf, but only for the sake of the passion and the words. Finally, there was so much fuss that they brought in a peasant from Volta who said: "That's the general. He read us his books." The trial lasted six months. There were protests. After his execution, as I have said, they sold more than a hundred kilos of clippings from his curly, jet-black, violet-scented hair. I saw one of these locks at the house of the kind young woman's grandchild.

A somewhat similar thing happened on the same spot in 1943 to one of the eighty thousand former English prisoners wandering about northern Italy after Mussolini's overthrow. But this man was no romantic: he did not stay to suffer his destiny but escaped. No one sold his hair.

Ten kilometers out of Brescia, from the Peschiera road, we had an excellent view of the Villa Ferraroli, one of the most beautiful in Italy. Although the sky did everything appropriate to a cheerful mood, I was reminded of Edgar Allan Poe. The style of the Villa Ferraroli was very dour. It was situated on the steep slope of a hill covered entirely in yews. Their foliage was almost black. This effect had been heightened by the addition of some very beautiful cypresses laid out in very precise rows and enclosing a staircase more than a hundred meters wide and three hundred long. In the distance it looked exactly like a ladder, but I could not say whether the stone was marble. It seemed that it was not, for they had found that an unsatisfactory alternative. They must have searched for and discovered the kind of white stone that would provide a perfect contrast to the dark green foliage. At no point was there any trace of the reflection you would expect from marble. The black of the leaves had been allowed to give the scene a finishing touch. The white was matte, and quite without depth. The effect was extraordinarily striking. The villa was located at the top of the ladder, which therefore led not to the gallows but to a very charming and handsome place in the seventeenth-century manner. The architects in this area were philosophers.

The surroundings of the Vila Ferraroli and the little town

of Rezzato were sheer Poussin. I saw very fine russet-red, almost purple farms with porticoes, set on the summits of hills among green oaks. Almost everything built of stone appears sacred. I never saw a standard so majestic as the simple laundered sheet that I saw hanging to dry from a window in Rezzato.

As we drew closer to Lonato, the country began to look increasingly familiar. The road wound through a rough, even bristly landscape. It was covered with acid-green reeds that occasionally revealed the pink earth of the fields. Oxen with vast horns were drawing wagons over the crossways. The apple orchards were so heavily planted that they were like the thickets of pleasure groves in medieval illuminations. The rows of haricot beans, string beans, peas, lettuce, and cabbage were arranged along meadows and stubble fields that were no bigger than handkerchiefs but endlessly recurrent, like the squares on a chessboard. The farms were clearly big enough for three or four people, and no more. Here a mulberry tree proffered its shade. Then there was a vine. And there some eggplants and pumpkins were drying on a low wall. Now five or six tomatoes on a plate. Then a yellow melon. Bottles of wine were left to cool in the irrigation canals. This was the countryside of Virgil's *Georgics*. The poet's birthplace, Mantua, was twenty kilometers to the south. The medieval and fifteenth-century buildings of Lonato rose out of the gardens about the town.

After Lonato we could see Lake Garda sparkling beyond the fields. At first we (or rather I) found the lake excessive. It seemed to add a vulgar note to everything, with its cafés and fried foods, its bars, and its terraced restaurants with sunshades.

But the lake opened out when we left Desenzano. We drove along grassy banks and the air smelled pleasantly of fish.

Inevitably, where the water extended for more than a few square kilometers, the banks attracted mediocrity. Nevertheless, Lake Garda (like the sea) was undeniably majestic. There was no iodine in the air, but the wind blew without hindrance over the bare waters. The great lakes and the sea are ready-made images and reminders for those who cannot picture freedom in any form. Perhaps a lake like Garda is even slightly superior to the sea in this respect, for it is somehow more intellectual. At any rate, Catullus, the ancient Roman poet, and Carducci, the poet of a unified Italy, came to live near this lake. Can Grande della Scala (the "Big Dog," on the basis of the pun Can=*cane*=dog), warlord, ruler of Verona, and patron of the arts, had a castle built here where Dante stayed. There were grottoes for them here, or they liked to spend time on the decorative rocks at the far end of Sirmione, which was almost an island. I am thinking of Carducci here, but Dante also liked a theatrical setting. Mussolini set up the vicious yet ineffectual Republic of Salo on the opposite bank after his overthrow, and under German protection. I had noticed before how vast expanses of water reflect a white light from the sky that is conducive to dreams, but also to grotesque visions. Scantily clad typists from Milan were pedaling water-tandems together with their bosses.

We arrived in Peschiera, which by now did not seem at all surprising. It was a formidable Italian citadel and one of the corner bastions of the famous "Quadrilateral Fortress" of Lombardy. It looked like a finely chiseled chess piece. The lawn of the counter-scarp in the fortress wall was fit to grace an Oxford college, and the moat was a *canaletto*. The drawbridge groaned under our 4 CV before the walls swallowed it up. Within the town everything was minuscule apart from the toys of war. The houses and shops were so narrow that you would easily recognize an inhabitant of Peschiera in the Antipodes, for he would never dare to make a broad gesture, but look to see if there was room enough behind his elbow before taking out a pocket handkerchief. I was intrigued to note that the postcards here were half a centimeter smaller than anywhere else. This only goes to show that you can find traces of sublimity even in a grocer's shop. But there were also the fortifications.

These fortifications were certainly impressive, and I would counsel anyone who visits them to read the *Memoirs* of General Govone.

On 10 April 1848, Govone, then a lieutenant in General Bes's brigade, which was besieging Peschiera, defended by the old Austrian General Rath, was sent to the town as a negotiator. He asked for the surrender of the fortress. This was a purely conventional request, between officers and gentlemen. The intention was to give the commander of the garrison at least an opportunity to answer that he was an old and honorable soldier, and that he would not destroy his reputation toward the close of his career. Rath did not refuse the chance to do exactly that, and added a short speech on the changing fortunes of war. But now Govone must speak for himself about those famous fortifications.

"I remounted my fine Prussian horse. The wind was fresh and gentle. The sun had appeared in the east. I was in love. The memory of my affection for this wonderful distant landscape, which I was actually looking at for the first time; the promise of a campaign that had begun so well; the possibility that I had earned a certain glory in combat with the enemy, and that my parents and my bride might already have heard of this: all this moved me so deeply at that moment that I would not have exchanged these dreams even for the entire lifetime of a peaceful and sybaritic monarch.

"When General Bes learned of General Rath's refusal, which he had not really expected, he wrote immediately and with dismay to his headquarters, saying that the fortress intended to resist an attack, and that he must be sent the heaviest possible pieces of artillery without any delay.

"At daybreak on 13 April our batteries were in a position to open fire on Peschiera. In the meantime, the king, who insisted on sharing all the glory and hazards of the troops, had given the order to await his arrival before beginning the onslaught.

"I left at a gallop. In Monzambano I wrote to General Franzini and sent the despatch by a hussar, who immediately sped off to Volta. A few minutes later, however, I also rode to Volta and arrived at the very moment when the hussar was handing over the letter. Signor Salasco and Signor Franzini, whom I met with first, told me that General de Bormida and the Duke of Genoa had already left with the order to open fire; that the king was now mounted and ready to proceed to Peschiera; and that I was to accompany him fifty paces ahead of the commanders' advance until we came in sight of the objective. I was burning with impatience to get into the thick of things, and I decided to lead the king along the main road.

"We were hardly at Ponti when I left the headquarters company without a word; our batteries had not even started to fire and I was anxious to warn General Bes of the king's arrival at Ponti, and to tell him that he was authorized to commence firing.

"For five hours, fourteen heavy cannon spewed out a storm of balls and shells. General Bes went from battery to battery, and then to the forward position of a company of Swiss volunteers, encouraging everyone by his words and example. We were near the Swiss when General Bes saw that all our cannonballs were merely striking the ramparts. He told me to inform the artillery officers.

"I could take two routes: one under cover and protected; the other direct and quick in comparison, but entirely in sight of the enemy. I was so aroused by everything I saw that I took the shortest way to the first battery. I heard two or three balls from flintlocks or the sharpshooters on the ramparts whistle past my ears and embed themselves in the ground a few steps in front of me. I was proud to know that they were expending these shots on me. I had been just as proud during the preceding days of the honor of attracting a number of bullets when I was on my way to enter the positions of our batteries on the maps. The batteries were under construction, and the information would allow the correct distance and elevation to be calculated. But now a bomb burst above my head and split a tree in two. Although one half of the bomb disappeared harmlessly, a fragment struck the ground near my horse's hoof. The fright upset it for a moment, but it soon recovered.

"After five hours' firing, which eventually succeeded in eliminating a few of Fort Salvi's cannon, the king proceeded to the Cascina Recchiano, General Bes's headquarters. While His Majesty was on his way into the courtyard (where he rapidly held a council of war and decided to send another negotiator into the town), a cannonball hurtled through the door, passed a few centimeters over the king's head, and penetrated one of the windows of the house.

"The plenipotentiary departed. He was Baron La Flèche, a captain attached to the general staff. He approached the fortress holding a white flag, but as the fire continued and they (somewhat angrily, it seemed) directed a hail of grapeshot at him, he turned back. I asked General Franzini's permission to go myself, but he said that it would be sheer insanity.

"Since it was now quite evident that the Austrian general was unwilling to surrender, the king ordered our side to cease fire, remarking that this implied no loss of honor, for we had attacked the fortress in conformity with the rules of war, and there was no reason to prolong the attack."

We were ravenous at the thought of the fried fish listed on the menus of the restaurants in the little harbor, and sat down to eat on the quayside, in the open air. The water from the lake reached the fortress moat and ditches, creating miniature harbors where little gondola-shaped boats were already afloat. We were positioned at the entrance to one of these minor waterways, flanked by "ramparts both fine and firm," as Dante puts it. The lake breathed, so to speak, through these inlets and thus provided us with welcome fresh air. We ordered white wine, which they said came from Mantua. And the canal nearby was the Mincio. I imagined it covered with swans (but I had confused it with the Serpentine in London's Hyde Park). Its water was quite transparent, and the bed was carpeted with algae of some size; their movement was so captivating that I could have watched it forever.

Finally, they served up an atrocious meal. It was white fish dipped in a pan of boiling oil (linseed oil, you would have thought). In general, not only in Peschiera or Italy, people are bad at frying fish. They turn the fish into something horribly golden-brown and crispy instead of making sure that the flesh stays tasty and juicy. This is my recipe: put only a little (olive) oil in the pan. As soon as it starts to seethe, put the fish in, and fry it first on one side, then on the other. Then it will remain white, soft, and juicy. Serve it with the oil that has mixed together with the juices from the fish. If you use this method, even sardines are delicious. Fish always taste of the water they live in. Each river has its own particular qualities. These can scarcely survive a process akin to cooking salsify almost rigid in castor oil. I have known people to reject some freshwater fish because they tasted of sewage. They were quite right to do so when they had been served up something out of a chamber pot seasoned with boiled peanut oil. But even a tincture of sewage is delicious if you wash the fish so thoroughly first that you leave it with only the least trace of pee odor, especially if the juice of the fish is mixed in, and there's the additional aroma of a slightly fruity olive oil. Eat it in the open air that smells as the fish tastes, alongside the water it came from, and the pleasure will be indescribable. You should try everything. Happiness demands effort. Experience and imagination have their parts to play, and bring their rewards. The fish in Peschiera was merely a certain means of conveying to my mouth a certain quantity of (bad) oil that had been cooking on the stove for an hour. They had slaughtered a hundred thousand minor tastes, a hundred thousand opportunities of enjoyment and even wonder, a hundred thousand images of delight waiting to emerge beneath my tongue. There was no point in fishing if that was the pathetic outcome. You could get the same results with bread crusts or a piece of sponge cut in the shape of a fish.

I was surprised that Italians could produce anything like that. They are usually excellent cooks. The woman who served us was clearly from Peschiera, but she certainly had no part in the cooking. I looked into the kitchen. Everyone there came from Peschiera, but I saw what was wrong. They were Italians, but Italians intent only on making money.

We were bloated without having eaten properly. Even my pipe tasted woebegone, which surely had something to do with that unreal afternoon light. The lake was chalky white, and the sky was white too. It was very difficult to throw off the feeling of constriction this gave us. Four thin, indeed gaunt, sweaty priests were leading a dusty party of orphans along the quays, where there was nothing to see. A bovine-faced little boy hand in hand with a little girl (probably his sister) brought up the end of the column. They were all tired and sleepy. They needed reassuring, to be told they would soon be all right. Buses were arriving and would soon discharge their tourist cargoes to eat the fried fish.

Beyond Peschiera the road ran between steamy gardens and orchards. They lay between us and the marshes of Mincio, where the mists came from. Around the time when Govone was engaged in the attack on Peschiera in accordance with the rules of conflict, peasants in these marshes were waging their own war on mail coaches and even companies of mounted gentry. They killed out of fear and above all a lack of self-assurance. "We don't know how to talk to people," they explained, "and anyway, what would we say to a well-dressed gentleman when we've just stopped him at gunpoint? How could we tell him nicely that we want to go and drink wine in Mantua? He would say that had nothing to do with him. We don't want to stand there like idiots." Later on there would be utterly bizarre private discussions with priests after they had confessed *quite frankly* to very weighty crimes. "If only we knew how to put things," they would say, yet they were quite capable of speaking lucidly in the confessional. In short, they were in search of a philosophy of life.

Apparently the grandfather of a friend of mine escaped from these philosophers' clutches by imitating Sheherazade in the *Arabian Nights*. They were just starting to press the heavy triggers of their ancient flintlocks when he uttered a few words that sounded like the beginning of a story. They put the guns down to ask him how it went on. When it came to it, these frightened peasants were bored. They were much more interested in entertainment than in robbery. But remember who they were: unimaginative people for whom killing was an exciting release from the usual dreary run of things. Though of course they might have been just stupid, as their conversation with the priest would seem to suggest. They couldn't carve a statue of a saint from a block of wood, but on countless occasions they had seen a meadow that in the fog looked like something more than a meadow, and made them scratch their heads. That was why they tried their luck, blocked the road, and threatened travelers with their flintlocks, just to see what might happen. Of course they liked listening to stories. They would murder women as easily as men, but stopped short at rape; there were no atrocities. All the same, they polished off some really beautiful creatures who might well have struck a bargain with them. And they never stole more than loose cash. Money chests still crammed full of gold coins were found afterward, quite intact. All they had ransacked was their victims' pockets. The odd thing was that they had a leader, which makes you think.

We were going to Verona to see the Princess of Trebizond and the horse market. The first was at the Basilica of Saint Anastasia and the second must be all over the town. There were said to be six thousand horses at the fair. Antoine had been a cavalryman, a sergeant in fact. In 1940, when France was broken and defeated, and the main highways were packed with refugees, he went home quite peacefully on horseback, along minor roads. He was very excited at the thought of six thousand horses in a single city. I also looked forward to the experience. And then there was Juliet's balcony.

Antoine's driving when he entered a strange town was quite admirable. He turned left and right without hesitation, and with an assurance that made everyone breathless, particularly the locals. When leaving Rigaste San Zeno, he turned right (whereas I was sure that the town was to the left), and into a broad, dramatic but empty street. It was still the time of the midday siesta. Here again we thought we were in Brescia, but in the daytime. The low, scarcely single-story houses were neatly arranged; their fronts were obviously "Italian"; and the perspectives of the streets were exactly like those in all the illustrations in manuals explaining the laws of perspective in geometrical terms (even the telephone wires seemed to imitate ruled and badly rubbed out vanishing lines). The mortar on the walls was so bright, the definition of sun and shadow so precise, and the exact center point of the background in compliance with the golden mean so nicely occupied by a triple-arched gateway in the Romanesque style that we were convinced that we were entering a stage set once again. But there was no one to be seen. Perhaps it was a day without rehearsals. Only a handsome white and certainly very intelligent greyhound, whom they had forgotten to tell about the day off, had arrived to play his part and was walking about, utterly bored. When the theater opened they would surely put on a play about the Big Dog (Can Grande della Scala again). We were at the Corso Porta Palio. We had to turn around. I was right, of course: now the town was straight in front of us. Antoine said it was very easy to find your way when you had a plan of the city, and I had one; and furthermore, what we had just seen was well worth the effort. I had to agree. All I wanted to point out was that Verona was on the left when leaving Rigaste San Zeno, to give the truth its due. After all, it was only proper to do so, even when traveling. Antoine agreed. He merely wished to remind us that, without any map, and relying on his own normal, unaided intuition (which he seemed to claim was a kind of electrical current that acted abruptly and without warning on your wrists at the driving wheel), he had brought us right up to sights which were well worth the trouble. I agreed. I merely wanted to point out—given what we now knew were Antoine's normal intuitions—that it would possibly be advisable to find an object of some kind, whether wood or metal, a charm, say, that might protect us from his *abnormal* intuitions. I had noticed—not here, but from time to time elsewhere—certain monster trucks that seemed very contemptuous of intuitions of either kind. There was also the matter of no-entry signs. Antoine's only riposte to this was that you had to die some-time, so that it was well worth ignoring all the no-entry signs now and making sure you had seen everything that *wasn't* in the guidebooks. I agreed. But I still thought that my idea of looking for some kind of amulet wasn't as silly as all that. After all, we were in the land of amulets, and we should take advantage of this.

We had not seen a single painting, either oil or fresco, since arriving in Italy. The landscapes we had passed through, of course, had been by Poussin, Giambellino, Giorgione, Conegliano, Bellini, and even Giotto, and yes, even Tiepolo (I am thinking particularly of *Angelica e Medoro nella capanna dei pastori*), in that order. On the street we had seen figures from Raphael (though not from Michelangelo), but they wore ele-gant modern clothes and surrealistic hats. The villages had contributed their chickens and their still-lifes by Crivelli. I went to Castel Vecchio to see Stefano da Zevio's *Madonna*.

She sat in a Persian garden. You could scarcely credit the rich quality of the little priest's garden where the Virgin was sitting. It was as narrow as a coffin and enclosed in walls decorated with the arabesques of espaliers and ivy trees. I am not a skilled interpreter of pictures. It is an art form that I began to understand (if at all) late in life. I know that an overcast white sky can touch a summer afternoon with tragedy. There were five or six *tiny* angels waiting for who knows what among the plants in Our Lady's garden. They looked like minute shrew mice ready to scamper off at the least movement. The Child on the Virgin's knee was very nice and jolly, and as chubby as you could wish. He had what all mothers like so much: dimpled knees and elbows. At the foot of the picture a sad-looking woman with the same features as the *Madonna* had a wreath of everlasting flowers tucked over one of her otherwise empty hands.

When I talk about a painting, I worry about not hitting off the effects of the colors, for that is the most important aspect. I can simply mention red, green, blue, and yellow, but these words convey nothing visual. I have noticed that clever commentators overcome this inadequacy by resorting to metaphors. This seems to satisfy everyone. But can anyone say they have *seen* a picture when it is described for them in words? To depict it in terms of feeling (which seems better at first) is confusing in the end. The truth is, you need a universal alphabet to express the impact of a painting. Stefano's *Madonna* made me think of the meadows of Monte Viso in full flower (which gave me a similar pleasure). But who was present in the meadows of Viso on 6 July 1915 at exactly the same time as me, in precisely the same light, in exactly the same state of mind, and with exactly the same angle of vision? The ideal person would also have to have been twenty years of age, a private soldier in the 159th Alpine infantry regiment, in a company commanded by a good sergeant, have come to a halt and be as hungry as a wolf, have opened a tin of sardines in oil, like sardines in oil, be sure that there was a good hour's rest for his feet, and know that there was still a full month to go before leaving for the front. Not to mention the letter from home which I had received the day before, and the money order inside it. A particularly good friend was also sitting next to me, and it was ten o'clock exactly. (By half past ten the situation was quite different, for the wine in my canteen had turned quite sour on the march.)

The Princess of Trebizond was at the back on the right in a corner of the Basilica of Saint Anastasia, high up there in a vault, but so high that she was not so attractive as I had expected. The wear and tear to this fresco that allowed the mother-of-pearl ground of the wall and the rich reddish brown of the stone to gleam through the pure tones increased the special magic of the image. In the overall gold there were a few touches of pink (some of the rooftops in the town), violet (the sky seen through the trees in the wood), and red (the cover under the horse's saddle). All these were like cloves in a meal (if you like cloves and they suit that particular dish). I particularly like Pisanello's drawings (I always understand drawings more than paintings). For a long time I had used four or five (black and white) reproductions of *Saint George and the Princess of Trebizond* as bookmarks. Now I could actually see the face in color: her high Breton forehead, that strong nose, those sensual yet somewhat disdainful lips, that shapely ear, and that imposingly trussed-up hair, painted in the same bright yellow tones as the shimmering golden mountains in the background. Her face had the typical complexion of a captive now free at last. Saint George on the other side of the

AN ITALIAN JOURNEY

horse was almost as pale. He too had not a drop of blood left in his veins, in spite of his hammerhead shark's mouth. Was he getting down from the horse, or was he about to swing back into the saddle? Nothing was more unadorned than the face of the princess. The situation in the greenish-bronze thickets where the scene is set looked rather tense. That was obvious from the woman's eye, and her slightly erased hand.

Now we had to find the horse market. The streets near Saint Anastasia were weirdly entangled. We tried to follow our noses: six thousand horses must be traceable. But there was nothing of that kind, only the odor of a southern town in the sun. Verona smelled of ripe melons. The only riders we met with were those taking the air astride their chairs in the doorways. Finally, we asked people. "There isn't any autumn horse market," they told us, smiling. "There isn't one till March. The autumn one is advertised in the stations, hotels, brochures, and posters just in case we decide to have two." In fact, all they wanted to do on that heavy thundery autumn day, from the Grassmarket to Castel Vecchio, from Romeo's house to Juliet's house, was to make their siesta last as long as possible.

I could understand this. You would never think that the man who gave us this information (a watchmaker, I think; in any case, he wore a blue smock and was sitting in front of a watchmaker's shop), in the Via Trotta, had finished his siesta. He slept sitting upright, he slept with his eyes open, and he spoke as if our conversation were but part of his little afternoon dream. We had also noticed that the bedrooms in southern countries, and therefore Italian bedrooms (I don't mean hotel rooms, but private, marital, bedrooms), were furnished quite minimally and with anything to hand (except for the bed). There was often only a bed and a chair, or a bed and a night table, or a bed and a vase. I remember one with merely a bed and a wire with a harsh, naked electric lightbulb at its end hanging from the middle of the ceiling. We had also noticed that all bedrooms were "at the back": that is, they looked out on a courtyard, an alley, or a cul-de-sac. They were never rooms with a view, for what use was that? It isn't the view that entices you into a bedroom, and the pleasure you seek there cannot be wrung from a nice piece of furniture. (This, of course, would delight Italians with their liking for double entendres: for them a "nice piece of furniture" is also a woman who is certainly good-looking but [alas!] irredeemably stupid.) Sleeping, even if you had flitted from one bedroom to another, sleeping when all was said and done, was a very serious matter there: above all sleeping in the daytime, for that meant wealth, well-being, and importance. Only a gentleman slept during the day. Such a man deserved to be greeted, respected, and *feared*. It was not the active revolutionary who impressed people but the man powerful enough to *sleep in the daytime*, a man whom no one dared disturb. There was good reason to be careful in this respect, for someone who could afford to be asleep could master, dominate (or wipe out) everyone else around, or was unusually brave (which came to the same thing). Pisanello should have painted his Saint George in a deep sleep. Ariosto's heroes are often asleep. A man who sleeps during the day (and you have to imagine him in a bedroom with no more than a bed and a naked lightbulb) is unquestionably a hero. He despises love, and all pleasures and debauchery, if he is not their unique origin. He scorns trade and industry, politics, plots and power. This clearly indicates immense power or vast courage. At any event, he is a gentleman.

Now we were in apolitical Verona at last. I was convinced that we had arrived in the middle of the major autumn horse market, though there seemed to be many, many more than the six thousand horses referred to in the posters in stations, in the hotel literature, in the tourist brochures and guidebooks. There were thousands and, it seemed, hundreds of thousands, of horses galloping through the sleeping heads of Verona. But we forgot the market and thought only of the pleasure of slipping quietly along the cool alleyways, between the houses with tight-closed shutters. Through half-open doors we peered into deserted shops packed with rolls of cloth for suits, alarm clocks, cigars, spirits, or engravings of Trieste as it was in 1842. History is often a matter of odds and ends.

Finally we crossed the Adige and set our sights firmly on Vicenza. It was already very late. That day, clearly, they had been forced to prolong the siesta in Verona because of the extreme heat and the thunderclouds. The light was unreal. We were enclosed, so to speak, within the arches of a heavy vault of cumulus. In spite of the chugging of the engine, we could sense the great silence all about us. We passed (submissively yet peaceably) between two rows of poplars unmoved by any breeze.

I had heard (but accidentally: for they spoke vaguely, by intention, using terms they thought I could not decipher) the story of a "priest." That is the word they used for anyone who legally enforced the always hypocritical injunctions of political parties. I shall not relate this particular anecdote because it was told by "us" about "them," and "they," whoever we or they may be, can never act with courage or good faith.

We drove on through poplars, and here and there through meadows, in an area of hills almost like real mountains. It was through these hills that the later disgraced Napoleonic General Moreau pursued Wurmser's armies after certain military stratagems had worked at Arcole, Lenato, and Mincio.

Those were the first modern battles. It was no longer a matter of capturing provinces but of imposing a certain view of human happiness on your enemy. This was evidently the source of the daring that so disconcerted the Austrian generals. They tried to hold on to rivers and hillsides, whereas their opponents held on to ideas. Nothing was less helpful to the rapid advance of an army than these hilly places now outlined by the oblique light of the setting sun disappearing beneath dark clouds. The carrot of ultimate happiness has been held out to us since humanity left the Garden of Eden. It is an advantageous tool for all and sundry, for the mere promise of its eventual reign is enough. There is no difference between the happiness guaranteed by the Church and that which materialists assure us will be ours. It always lies in the future and we have to run after it, killing, killing, killing all the way, running amok in helpless, murderous frenzy like (so they say) the Malays. A tragic fate is reserved for those who want to remain free or who hold on to their own ideas: they are *thrown to the Christians.*

Vicenza was a romantic city. Like Verona, it had a Piazza dei Signori, but here the *signori* did not take their siesta (though, of course, it was almost night and, in any case, it was getting very dark). You had to be a quite innocent foreigner to believe that *signore* meant *seigneur,* or anything like a nobleman, as the guidebooks said, or that it had anything to do with Dante, Lamberti, Can Grande, or Scaligere surviving in monumental form in these geometrical purlieus of supremely exalted pride. *Signore* quite simply meant Mr. So-and-So, as in everyday usage, and referred to a hairdresser's assistant, bank clerk, shop cashier, wholesaler, mason, garage hand, or bar owner. Yet these people still went by the names Can Grande, Lamberti, and sometimes even Dante. They were all dressed in extraordinarily well-cut, bespoke suits. Here there was an eternal youthfulness, even childhood, in the sense that term had in the Middle Ages when they wrote of the infancy of Lancelot, or of William of Palerne, saved from poisoning in childhood by a werewolf. Neither old age, nor wretched poverty, nor married and family life with threateningly huge women could harbor half as many worries as the need to wear elegant, superior clothes and shimmering shoes. There was always something you could cut down on: food. You didn't go without it for any other reason, and certainly not if you had to dress so drably that you could keep your self-respect only by asserting that the cowl doesn't make the monk. This revealed a knowledge of the human heart unknown and inaccessible to any Greenlander (and there are Greenlanders even in Marseilles). It was a form of humility: the humility of those who know that without outward trappings they are nothing. These people were wise. Disillusionment hardly ever made them cruel. They had replaced horses with a little machine that sounded like a wasp and was in fact called a Vespa. These were their favorite vehicles, with which they gamboled and capered about the squares for fun and as a form of sexual display. But all this was reassuring and in the end a source of greater confidence in humanity than all so-called scientific discoveries and dead political slogans. While the gray party men were deciding the future of Europe, here people were holding on to their humanity. They did so in the only tolerable sense of the word: that which doesn't ask you to eradicate your neighbor (or only to a very limited extent!).

All the millionaires in the world seemed to have made appointments in these tortuous streets. Their faces were full of the heavy dignity and even sadness that I had noticed in Turin. But that did not mean that they were lamenting a lost paradise, or that they were intent upon the conquest of power. It was simply that they enjoyed big business. They had not chosen to be fervent participants in some mass gymnastic display (or to be onlookers at some spectacle in a vast stadium. For the same reason Italians as a whole do not need bullfights). Men and women alike were out walking, rubbing shoulders, sizing one another up, trying to impress one another, interacting. You had to know how to interpret every reaction correctly. Your life was at risk if you ignored the *real* meaning of a slight puckering of the mouth (when someone was also actually smiling). Some especially clever people (as easily young as old) knew that the most they risked was a wasted evening.

Since 1945 writers have been telling lies to look good in the right columns of papers owned by the self-declared guardians of the true faith. Henceforth, it is generally agreed, happiness is the concern of political theorists. I have often talked about happiness since being among those people who had no faith and, moreover, every possible defect.

Vicenza was surrounded by black-wooded hills. It was through these hills that the Austrian General Alvinczy marched his troops at lightning speed against Napoleon's commander, Massena. Alcinczy stole his opponent's master card and persuaded the Venetian peasants that he was bringing them democracy along with his cannon. The guns flew literally from hand to hand in the ravines of this mountainous region.

It was too late now to see Giotto's murals in Padua. We would do that on the way back from Venice. But now we would drive slowly to the sea, taking our time in the goldenblack twilight. Everything around us was worth seeing. The countryside had taken on a friendly peasant look. We were no longer in the opulent Virgilian approaches to Mincio. This was an area of easygoing people who did not take even the earth seriously. If there were poets among them, I was sure that they did not celebrate the corn or grape harvest, or the oxen with their lyre-shaped horns. As for lyres, a boy, neither handsome nor ugly, was playing a bugle in the doorway of a little farmhouse. He was practicing his scales; he was getting used to his instrument; he would try waltzes later on. But he already had the "right lips," as they said, and the sounds he drew from his little bugle were sweet and pure. They sometimes made me think of Don Quixote or, rather, of the landscape of his exploits.

On the way to the coast, people lost all trace of avarice and assumed a kind of nonchalance. The coastal areas proper clearly encouraged more passionate emotion. The sea was always there to prompt an irresistible longing for flight (more intense than the need to live in a social group), but a few kilometers inland was an Edenic garden of sensitivity, especially on these flat, muddy banks. There people were less subject to the drive to make money, but this made them intent— and how much more dignified that was—on enjoying life. There you had to be unusually determined to stay above the fray of fortunes made and lost, and to resist the temptation to enter the game.

Here they built themselves little farms more like huts of straw than of stone, though the Italians are enthusiastic masons. You could see only gardens, but no fields. Even the corn was grown like vegetables for which there was no urgent need. None of these houses had any kind of barn or hayloft. They all looked far too small for the number of people living in them. Under the vines round them there was always the same big, fat woman, dressed in red and surrounded by a great number of children in bright colors. In the hot part of the year, the men and women preferred to sleep outside where they felt less inhibited. No more than a hundred days a year were needed to cultivate this land and keep it neat and tidy. I saw little orchards with six trees planted so carefully that each of them was a work of art in its own right. All this was contained within an expanse of only thirty kilometers. Toward Padua the countryside regained its fullness. Saint Antony was honored in Padua. You had to pay for his intercession. You planted five rows of potatoes for the family and one for the saint (so, six altogether). But you stopped at the hundredth row. A pious farmer told me this, for he crossed himself all but imperceptibly as he spoke.

After Padua we took to the highway again in order to gain time in this area of marshes and rushes. As usual, it was late at night when we reached our first hotel. When we set out from France I was not anxious to see Venice: the thought of honeymoon weekends, Wagner, and d'Annunzio seemed as repellent as a thousand views of the place on postcards and in travelogues at the cinema. In spite of Byron, Stendhal, and Casanova—yes, even Proust—I wanted to leave Venice out. But the ladies insisted on seeing it. Now we were getting close. But of course (as I reassured myself), this was the Adriatic.

There was a little daylight left, and what I saw, even if only sand and marshland, was very satisfying. For me there is nothing attractive about places like Naples and Capri. The exquisite azure blue bores me as much as the rocks and flowers. I don't need set pieces but landscapes undisturbed by the sudden appearance of people with trays of potato chips or ices. Similarly, I dislike "meetings" of all kinds, whether they are designed to advance the happiness of nations or to promote culture or erotic delights. If there were three of us to enjoy a superb view, the other two had to be my friends.

IV

Venice

We reached Mestre in the middle of the night, but arc lights disclosed a vast oil refinery, the fairy-tale castle proper to our times. I am not inflexible. When people could not live without gods they erected a temple on every promontory, and in the age of diversion they built a little palace in every grove. Nowadays they construct dams and metal silos to store equipment. Even beauty, like the picturesque, is born of necessity and is never wholly disinterested. These huge aluminum-coated metal edifices resounded two or three octaves higher than anything that tradition had trained us to detect. The outcome was a highly nuanced feeling of unreality. The shape that applied mathematics has decided is apt to withstand a maximum force is as pure as all those forms which we admire "instinctively." At the edge of that dark lagoon, these tanks, these pipes, and even the vile stench which issued from them were elements in a tragedy that, some hundreds of years ahead, would seem part of "antiquity." We are already acquainted with Philoctetes and his malodorous, snake-bitten foot, and the best way to understand the punishment of Prometheus is to think of an autopsy carried out behind a graveyard wall on a scorching August afternoon. A while back I referred to Don Quixote with regard to a rustic trumpet;

the knight would not have balked at the oil refinery: he would have included it straightaway in his repertoire of lyrical tropes.

I preferred this spectacle to Millet's *Angelus*. As I did that of the vast buses "clad in the beauty of a thousand stars" that, as we made our way along the jetty, rumbled around us, crossed in front of us, overtook us, and, heaving their cargo from side to side, buzzed us at top speed. Only one thing frightened me: the thought of gondolas and of everything that implied.

We had reached a square—Autorimessa—where cars were parked. It contained easily a thousand cars in rows, and a huge garage with phosphorescent walls, for they were entirely of glass. You could see the vehicles within ascending ramps that spiraled up to the fourth story. That was surprising enough, but most astonishing of all was the silence.

The square was small (a little later I discovered that it was an island). Three attendants in dungarees inserted our car. They did this by hand and very adroitly, so that the vehicles were literally stuck together. Autorimessa was lit only by small, dimmed electric lamps. The real light came from a large café terrace (with no customers at that time; it was nine o'clock), or was supplied by the radiance of the immense glass garage. In the half-light we could make out a few low-built old houses like those you find in Pietro Longhi's drawings.

Complete silence reigned. Mechanics, waiters, two Capuchin monks, and a group of eight people masquerading as German tourists in feathered hats were moving along slowly, as in a slow-motion picture, and speaking in subdued tones. Instinctively, the four of us also began to do everything slowly. This was like a game and unusually comforting. We could hear the water lapping.

We were hungry. Considering the time that our reduced

speed now demanded even to take out a handkerchief, it seemed that we would never find a restaurant in these dark and watery wastes. The canals I knew from books and paintings seemed like a fisherman's net in which we had been taken and were now held prisoner. I glanced apprehensively at the German tourists and the Capuchins who had been caught like us, but was then seized by the ghastly suspicion that they were not real.

Antoine decided to reconnoitre the area of the Pietro Longhi houses. He returned immediately, accompanied by a dwarf. He was a dwarf who had everything; at any rate, he had restaurants enough and to spare. He described all the restaurants that he could make available to us. He had round ones, long ones, square ones. "He's already offered me his mother, his sister, his brother, and a cardinal," Antoine said, more disillusioned than I had ever seen him.

It was the women who decided to trust the dwarf (as in chronicles of chivalry). He rejoiced at this and bowed to them, then made them a speech in which, in spite of all our concerns, I could not help noticing three or four extremely obscene words. Yet: "Live pure, speak true, right wrong, follow the Dwarf!" Another surprise: as soon as we left the parking lot we were walking through grass. Then we had to descend a slope, as if we were right out in the country.

As yet, I had not uttered a word. Accordingly, as far as the dwarf was concerned, I was the only one of our company he still had to beguile. Antoine had accosted him (or he had accosted Antoine); the women had accepted him; now he took me in hand. We passed by a house dimly lit from within. He told me to take care not to go in there, for it was an absolutely disgusting place, very, very poxy and *anticuore* (literally "anti-heart": in fact, a tumor of the horse's breast, though the word had a pleasant ring at that time of the day). "Monsignor," he said, addressing me as if I were a reasonably high ecclesiastic. He stuck close to me and made sure I was listening attentively, which kept us behind the others. "Monsignor, *guarda!*" He made an esoteric sign with his thumb and index finger: "*Fica,* very small, *fica.*" He was, he said, the king of very small *fica.* Tight little cunt, yes, people always wanted that. It was *inverzele,* he claimed (that is, "marbled," which told me that he was a Paduan. Butchers called meat "marbled" when it was red veined with white, a sign of excellent quality). He had found tight little cunt for all the great men: Churchill, he said, and Guynemer. Guynemer, the French air ace in World War I who died in 1917? Yes. He pretended his little arms were a bird's wings, and flapped them. One is always inclined to treat dwarves as children, but this one (his head was at the height of my waist) was an old dwarf. He might well have been operating in Guynemer's time. I remarked that with his references he must do well. He told me not to worry, that for their part the ladies wouldn't be bored, you could trust him. Then, at high speed, he rolled out a catalogue of all the pleasures on offer.

But he had led us to a bridge across a little canal, and on the other side I saw an undistinguished little restaurant that looked perfectly adequate. Of course he immediately pronounced it to be syph-ridden and horse-tumorous, but we made it clear that we intended to go there just the same. It certainly wasn't the kind of place you would recommend to tourists. Nevertheless, we sat down at an outside table on the canal bank, from which we could see the little bridge over which shadowy figures were slowly passing. The dwarf had gone. We had lost him. He had disappeared as soon as the restaurant owner came out. We were served a heap of fried shrimps. For at least thirty years I had been waiting to eat fried shrimps again. My mother cooked them like that when I was a boy, but since then I had always been given ghastly boiled shrimps. Rediscovering your youth in a little restaurant is enough to turn it into a heavenly mansion. And the wine was delicious. The shrimp bowl was refilled enthusiastically and smilingly. It was a cool evening, we were surrounded by a town of divers, and, as it happened, the canal we were sitting by smelled strongly of iodine.

We were in an almost deserted area. We could see the waterways and stone-paved alleys vanishing into the distance under minute lamps. Our little eating place was tucked in between two houses with fine iron balconies. A little further off, in a shop that was still open, a notice said: "Blinds repaired." The tools for these repairs could be seen there in the light of a jet lamp. There were anvil blocks, blacksmith's hammers, a bench vice, files, and a kind of saucepan rack from which hung chains, burglar's pliers, wrenches, and shining bars and blades. The repairer of blinds himself was taking the air. He was a huge man with the face of a Turk and as bald as a galley slave. He sat astride a chair that cracked at his least movement. But he made hardly any: just enough to be entertained by a tame magpie perched on his shoulder and pecking at his arms. Shadows passed on the bridge and, on the distant waters, it was probably boats that we heard puffing, as they went by with a wash that stirred even the water in our canal.

Apart from this gasping, the magpie's little cries and the Turk's snorts, all was quiet. The customers in the restaurant were as silent and self-contained as prisoners slipping out of jail. We could detect the sound of wine being poured into glasses, and the noise of spoons and forks scraping and striking plates and the oil bubbling in the pan and then sizzling twice as fervently when the shrimps were thrown in.

I had already tasted the silence of deserts and the quietude of the high seas. They were both excessive. Once the first moment of happiness was spent, and as soon as my curiosity was reawakened, fear began to take hold of me. Obviously this was also a source of pleasure, but demanded an effort that exhausted me sooner or later. Leaving myself aside, I have known other people unusually endowed with this rare form of courage: people who dared to enjoy things. After the silence of a mountaintop, they would sigh with relief as the familiar grinding of street-car wheels at a curve in the rails pierced their consciousness.

The silence of Venice could effortlessly afford enough (far from banal) pleasure to last a lifetime. But it also had something that allowed it to be ranked with the truly great silences. Since disembarking (a term that fits the event precisely) at Autorimessa, I had realized why in all times and places so many worthy people had fled the world. It was something that might be defined thus: a sensibility that rarely delivers pleasure will provide it eventually. There is music, of course, but it is contrived, however beautiful it may be. We approach it as if it were an essence. We can listen to it only in weak doses: for an hour or two, at the most. Beyond that, for ten hours, for instance, the most beautiful melody would be sheer torture. We would no longer taste and enjoy it but become dead drunk, as if we had taken too much absinthe. The joys of looking are different. There is no need for the Parthenon or for Vézelay. Think only of the women you meet: a mouth, a nose, hair, sometimes just the face, whole and entire, or the breasts, the way this or that one walks, or

AN ITALIAN JOURNEY

their coloring, and here I am thinking just of those with no unique qualities. Flowers, trees, landscapes, animals, horses: visual emotion never reaches the highest pitch because our eyes are surfeited with possibilities. You cannot compare any visual emotion to that, for example, afforded by a beautiful voice. The ear is more sensitive because noise scarcely ever offers it an opportunity for pleasure. When it does so, our hearing takes its pleasure with vitality untried and undiminished, ready to run the whole gamut of sensation. Because instinct tells them this, the deaf are usually sad. They have lost a paradise they have scarcely apprehended: more than a paradise—veritable rapture.

How happy a blind person would be in Venice!

After supper we went to the landing stage that creaked on the other side of the bridge, and waited for the *vaporetto*. I asked for four places for San Zaccaria, as I had been advised to do by a girl who had started a conversation with me about our bags. To get all our things into the little 4 CV, we had not taken cases but stuffed our impedimenta into any empty space. I only had a beach bag that held my books and notebooks. But now, to move on, we had had to tie up my washing and Elise's in a scarf, and to cram things into the pockets of the coat I had over my arm. Antoine was similarly burdened. We were also very cheerful. This was enough to invite an impromptu conversation with anyone. The girl I had been talking to had warned me in a very pretty voice that I was about to lose a hand towel. We would certainly find a hotel in San Zaccaria, she said.

The puffing noise I had heard earlier now warned us that the *vaporetto* was about to arrive. The floating stage we were waiting on pitched beneath our feet as it approached. We could have been right out at sea. It was easier to embark than to get on a bus elsewhere, but as soon as we were on board we realized that, however small it was, it was a boat for all that, with all the usual dread possibilities. Indeed, we were risking everything, merely to tackle ten meters of water scarcely one and a half meters deep. We felt we were on a substance with a wholly illusory supportive power. We were no longer on a pavement that could swallow nothing unless the devil intervened (which occurs very seldom). If you don't understand what I mean, you must study young lovers in Venice when they part after their evening trysts. The people I am thinking of are plumbers, building workers, or telegraph clerks: Bernardin de Saint-Pierre's Paul and Virginia, in other words (remember how Virginia drowns in the sight of Paul, as her ship nears the shore. One actually dies, but the other's heart is mortally wounded). One of these young Venetians is in the boat and the other is still on the pier. Consternation literally grips their faces. You never feel anything like this ultimate moment of moments in Paris or London, or anywhere on *terra firma*, where you know that if mechanical measures fail, as a last resort you can always run back and rejoin your lover. In Venice, however, a hundred definitive separations of this kind take place throughout the day. It is a source of unhappiness for everyone concerned. But since people are afraid of being made fun of, they attribute it to the air of the lagoons.

In about 1900, on the Place Saint-Michel in Marseilles, there was a boat that circled round a rockery island in a pool fifty to sixty meters in circumference. It was called "A World Tour." My father took me there to try it. Of course he stayed on shore. That was how I learned about the heartbreak of separation. It was very valuable, and my father was well aware of this. He put his white shirt on for the occasion and made

AN ITALIAN JOURNEY

sure that his little black tie was neatly knotted. This made him look very handsome. He was naturally good, and I suspect that on those days he was especially good, and intentionally so. As soon as I was hidden by the rocks of the little island, it seemed like the end of the world, as in Venice. It lasted only a minute, and the next turn on the pool brought my father back in sight. But loss is an experience of finality, and has nothing to do with time as such; its effects are forever. Once you have lost people, even if you find them you never forget that you can lose them again. When I disembarked, my father shook my hand as if I were now a man. As we left the Place Saint-Michel we assumed an air of almost total unconcern.

It is not by chance that even mountain folk portray death as a ship. Every day in Venice, whether they were moving on the waterways or they wished to be on the other side of a canal, they died a thousand minor deaths. You soon got used to it. Then the rest of the world was effaced, which was delightful indeed, and you became wholly nonchalant. Time is not money in the Elysian Fields. *Finita la Commedia;* the Divine Comedy has hastened to its culmination: why run now?

It is unjust to ascribe it all to the bad air of the lagoons, but there, when your spirit (like Venetians) rejected more lively sensations of pleasure or joy, and succumbed to daydreams and vague musing, and to the lure only of tender sentiments, then (like Venetians) you felt that you had passed through the final metamorphosis, and that heights and depths alike were in the past.

You have to see St. Mark's Square late at night, when the musicians at Florian's have packed up their instruments and gone. No one will trouble you if you are the last customer on the café terrace and stay till three or four in the morning. The waiter is used to this, and it is to his profit too. However slightly you resemble a Venetian, that is, behave like a sponge on the seabed (an easily acquired tendency), he will come and sit down by you. You can talk to him as to no one else. There is no longer any question of syntactical stratagems, for here not dissembling but mutual confession is called for, so that you cooperate in an ideal exercise of your ability to enjoy the world. I noticed the complete absence of verbs from such conversations. The word "Constantinople" was sufficient to describe the wind growling in the interstices of the campanile. It was usually around that time that the water welled up strongly from the foundations of the church. You could see it issuing from the vestibule. It formed a lake sometimes more than a meter deep and could fill out until it had to be bridged with planks more than twenty meters long. They told me that it was fresh water and did not come from the sea but from the part of the church known as the *Luogo segreto,* or the *Tribunale.* You could watch it moving outward. You felt you were in a world wholly subject to water; that a universal inundation was beginning; that the bridge was about to go under; and that total catastrophe was imminent. I based my attitude on the waiter's (there more than anywhere else, you had to avoid becoming a laughingstock). But the feeling of a general cataclysm, as that black water began to invade a deserted St. Mark's Square at three in the morning, was compulsive. At such times you had very obviously to put your feet firmly on the rungs of the chair opposite you. *Tribunale* was my waiter's term for this sudden flood that some people said was the sign of a powerful east wind in the Adriatic. He said that it came from the altar which the Doge Ordelafo Faliero and Prince Pietro Zani had embellished and which Andrea Dandolo had finally adorned with heavy gold, rubies, diamonds, emeralds,

AN ITALIAN JOURNEY

and pearls. "*Ma non si scuopre se non nelle maggiori sollennità*" (It appears only on major feast days), he told me. He explained later that this altar "acted all by itself," without any help from the priests. This black water entering St. Mark's Square and gradually inundating it should not be taken lightly. He said all this in even tones, without ever raising his voice, and in very few words. Though all the substantives are his, I have put in verbs and made up sentences.

He was from Modena. He had been in Venice for twenty years and had worked at Florian's for seven. At one time he had run a little bar-restaurant on his own account in the Rio Santa Sofia, behind the Ca'd'Oro. His mother was still alive, and in the Misericordia quarter. Every evening the air of the lagoon advanced to the Canal Grande, by way of the *darsena,* or harbor inlet, known as the Sacca della Misericordia. The raffia blinds flapped in front of the doors. The Jesuits had to have steel wires inserted in the hangings in the porch of the Sant'Apostoli. He liked sitting on the marble paving in the street and enjoying the fresh air. He had seven customers who kept him going all year round. Air cost nothing and fish not much more. He asked me if I liked stuffed cuttlefish. His girl-friend was a market gardener who plied her trade from a fruit and vegetable boat on the canal. All he had to do was to go to the parapet, and she passed him a courgette, a tomato, or a handful of lamb's lettuce. He carried on a flirtation with a woman who had a grocer's shop at the corner of Rio Terra, behind the synagogue. She was *casca,* that is, she had the feet and legs of an elephant. It was an illness that originated on the Dalmatian coast. She couldn't move. But you had to "accept her for what she was." She gave him the leavings from bags of rice. You had to chop up lettuce and chervil with a clove of garlic and lots of parsley. Parsley was very good for you: it made you walk nicely. As for the tentacles of little cuttlefish, you had to make sure they were cut up small. They couldn't be any bigger than a guinea fowl's eggs. You made a sauce with tomatoes, oil, and the raw livers of three or four fat mullet. In houses where they were used to eating stuffed cuttlefish there was always a little pot of *garbinella*. The word meant sleight of hand. It was a purée of Paduan fennel. You pounded big fennel leaves, the sort that grew on the edges of marshes, in brandy. Then you macerated this paste, as fine as pottery clay, in alcohol for months. You took a lump as big as a man's fist and thinned it down with white wine. Then you boiled some rice and let it soak up some of this white wine. Cuttlefish was the only seafood that required seasoning with nutmeg. That was because it fed on the milky slime that floated between the ebb and flow of the tide. It took a long time to stuff cuttlefish, but of course there was time and to spare. Then you cooked them in a pan, making sure that the oil didn't bubble. This wasn't frying; it was *sborare*. This meant something disgusting, but anyone close to a pan in which cuttlefish are being *sborare*-d wasn't interested in what the word meant. The streets were paved with marble in the Misericordia area. It was a good life along the four big parallel canals where the undertaker's boats from the San Michele cemetery were moored. The churches of San Alvise and Madonna dell'Orto tolled their passing bells in three tones. The dead went by in red boats, along the waterways hung with funereal violet, escorted by black-clad watermen singing passages from the Lamentations of Jeremiah. A little mollusk with a lemony taste grew on the water-steeped walls throughout this parish.

He had forgotten Modena. His heart was in Venice. Nothing was more beautiful, he said, than to saunter on an autumn evening from the Malibran theater to St. Mark's. The rain in Venice was delightful. Only foreigners believed in sunlight. The rain brought out the smell of the houses. He knew of cupboards packed with doublets, greatcoats, ceremonial headgear, and rapiers. If the two of us had the time tomorrow (but we did not), he could show me vast rooms where the windows were now all closed up and where beds with all four posters infested with beetles and devoured by rot had become as fragile as sand castles. You mustn't touch them. They were just putrid: athlete's foot all the way up to the canopy. They came from the time when everyone had been away fighting the Croats and Turks. They had brought back a smell of leather with them. He had never understood why the sailors then wore boots. Those little Paduan sandals, something like pumps, were much better. They made them from goatskin, which became butter-supple in Venice. That's what he wore himself; after all, a waiter's feet were the tools of his trade. When he'd started, he'd often been forced, even during the day, to lean against a column. He'd given up the little bar in the Rio Santa Sofia. He hadn't been able to keep it because of his dreams, at one point, of bigger things. But who could blame him? He stood up to the worst. He didn't like it if they played music at cocktail time. If you listened to it you could get depressed. Signor Medio, who wrote books, told him that in Ariosto the exhausted warriors leaned against tree trunks holding their shields as he held his tray. He regained his composure and thought of the Paduan sandals. The air in Venice wasn't salty; it had seaweed in it. That was what gave it its softening, relaxing effect. They thought a lot of him now. He was the one who served English people. There were often five tables of them. You had to show them that you knew how to work or they started speaking their own language. But he wasn't going to stop there. You couldn't see Venice. When the rain came from the Greek islands, its smell permeated the city. They still kept pepper and cinnamon in bedrooms a hundred years ago. Two or three people lived in the palaces with all their rooms and staircases. The men went to Albania and came back with Turkish trousers. The women put cloves in their linen chests. Courting them was like eating stewed beef. There were white girls who never went out. Unlike the women tucked away by the Mohammedans, the fair captives of Venice never grew fat. There were a thousand tales of titled young women who were still slim after thirty years of total seclusion in immense palaces. They scented themselves with musk and ate candied sugar. From the Palazzo Pisani opposite the Accademia to the Merceria, past the Fenice theater, you could go secretly from one house to another by hidden doors. They burned incense paper all the way along these passageways. These were the streets of a dark town with its own life and very pure tallow candles in candelabra. When they came back from Crete and Asia Minor, the young people found their way in, their pockets full of crystallized olives, Mandarin oranges, and rosaries from Jerusalem. When a serious event called for it, they used ropes and well-oiled pulleys to drop midwives into these mole's galleries. The November rain coming from Cephalonia teased the smell out of the walls. Nothing is more evocative than a smell. The waiter at Florian's and many others persuaded me that you could exist on nothing in Venice as long as you rented a *casin*—a little place—and learned to live like the locals. To look right, which is so important in the south, all you needed was fresh linen every day. In the local slang a gondola was known as a *zanzarin*, and a *zanzarin* was actually a man who affected a fine hairstyle. Both the most ignominious collector of cigarette ends and the busiest worker in the Arsenal had time to sit on one of the steps that went down into the Lagoon and to watch the boats passing. They were sharp enough to observe that with each stroke of the pole a gondola disturbed the water behind it like a *zanzarin* shaking his locks when he wanted to show off in front of the ladies. That was why the cinemas didn't do so well. The same was true of anything that cost so much elsewhere. Of course, there were restaurants for tourists where you could eat boeuf bourguignon, but the little bar-restaurant asked two hundred francs for the shrimps, and for the same price you could get fillets of sole three centimeters thick. They also made pasta to all the Italian recipes and in all the Venetian styles. What is more, it was a place where the East, not only of the Turks but of the Mongols, penetrated far into Europe. You could find the strangest cakes. You used the palm of your left hand as a plate. You didn't have the annoyance of having the foot of a silly little table between your feet or that of being served and assessed by a etiolated pastry with the heart utterly taken out of it by flakiness or whipped cream. You ate while walking along the street. Anyone who has never seen a real Venetian biting into a *schiappeto* (a mixture of fried pasta and Turkish Delight topped with cream) while strolling along the Corso Larga will never know how to jettison all those childish rules of behavior that prevent us doing what we really enjoy without worrying about what people will say. Clearly these people could be obdurate, no matter how sacred the issue involved. There was no pleasure, recorded or not, to which they were not daring enough to devote themselves wholeheartedly in the middle of the street and in broad daylight, if need be. This gave rise to a kind of constant, exquisite dread which was the literal opposite of boredom.

The location of this city surrounded by water and paved with water made it the only place in the world where you could wear black indefinitely, and where black stayed plain and pure. Trousers, shirt, and sandals of deepest black: what a splendid form of dress. Nothing is more cheerful. They also made a kind of black hat from varnished straw, flat with a wide rim, enlivened by a minute braid of green ribbon hanging from the back like a love-lock. They went everywhere dressed like that. As there was never any dust, this black outfit was superbly economical. Women had colored skirts and often something in bright yellow round their chests. It was difficult to wash clothes in Venice. The Lagoon water was no use for that. A man in black in search of adventure was a fine sight. In the summer, when the sunlight cut sharply into the darkness of the alleyways, you saw women in bright colors running along in the light as if each of them was acting out the flight of the terrified Klearista. When you got closer you saw in the shadows five or six men in black who had just offered their help. Then they disappeared into the general obscurity.

The ways of Venice were those of a southern region where even the definite was provisional. The great campanile in St. Mark's Square had already collapsed once, on 14 July 1902. There were two walls right up to the top, one within the other, and an earthen ramp ran between them. It wound upward in so gentle a spiral that a horse could ascend trotting all the way to the *logetta*, at a height of sixty-five meters. There were quite a few things in Venice like that stairway in the Campanile di San Marco. They had never taken a horse all the way up to the *logetta*, but it was all arranged so that it could be done, and even at a trot. They worked on the principle that

AN ITALIAN JOURNEY

you might suddenly have need of the most extreme sensations. Accordingly, you had to be ready for such an occasion and to prepare yourself for it with practical exercises, like soldiers and engineers. That was why there were so few real sins in Venice. The churches were cool places where it was quite normal to be absolutely untroubled. You saw the sacristan going from couple to couple. He was asking for his tip. Sometimes there were regulars waiting there who willingly agreed for the sake of general peace of mind to assume postures of consummate piety as they waited. Nevertheless, there was a repugnant and sinister atmosphere about some of the altars where relics were exposed in twisted ornamental settings decorated with shells. These odds and ends of bodies, some of which were visibly moldering, could only be warnings of death and judgment, heaven or hell. Fragments of jawbones, feet, fingers, and even a heart like a frog in a glass jar made the earth seem a paradise which you had to enjoy before you were cast out from it, but also made certain pretenses seem apposite. Looking for pleasure—which was a continuous pursuit, even while you were asleep—was known as *andare a Nuolo* (a dialect form of the verb *olire:* to smell good), which included a kind of obscene play on words involving both oil and smell. This sort of expression, which seemed almost cynical and yet betrayed a feverish anxiety, proved that there was no real sensuality in question. It was not unusual to see men beseeching and weeping, which would seem quite out of place anywhere else. But everyone knew that it merely indicated a form of curiosity like that of a little boy who had stuck his finger (if necessary his entire hand) in twenty pots of jam, without actually consuming any of them.

There was one thing all of them, even the women, were

very proud of and boasted about: virility. All oaths and all insults referred to it. They used it as Zeus wielded his thunderbolt. It was virility that ensured their preeminence, took them where they wanted to go, and avenged them. They were very disconcerted, one might even say on the verge of tears, if you were not in awe of it. That was something they could never understand. Admittedly, their showing off had extraordinary effects on the weaker sex. Venetian women were so surprised if they were not assailed in this way (which they were used to withstanding for all of five minutes), that they put up no resistance whatsoever to such indifference. In a bank where I was changing money I met a very beautiful Venetian woman whom I could not avoid looking at. She all but feather-dusted me with her long eyelashes for the space of a generous instant. There was no reason for me to compliment myself. She had merely seen me concentrating on adding up, in her presence, and this she found incomprehensible.

Many girls in Venice were anemic. They went to the abattoir to drink warm ox blood. You saw them in the morning, always looking very stylish. They had a glass in their handbag or a silver mug engraved with their initials. It was usual to give a cup of this kind to the daughter of the house, if you thought she looked wan. They waited by the beast being slaughtered, but without forming a line as you soon learned to do in England. A butcher's boy would pierce the artery and the blood would pour or even spring out. They had to be very nimble to fill the glass without smearing themselves. Insufficiently adroit novices were accompanied by their mothers. It had to be drunk immediately, and swallowed down all at once, followed by a grain of sea salt on the tongue. This tonic, it seemed, worked wonders. When I was there a glass of blood cost twenty-five lire, as well as the gratuity the butcher's boy shook under the ladies' noses before sticking his knife in the animal. The meat from a creature bled in this way wasn't so good, so it was said. The butchers tried to sell it at the same price as other meat, but women claimed to recognize it and called it *castrone*. Since the ox was already an ox, this was an untranslatable witticism, so it seemed.

People were still generous in Venice. It was impossible to know who was rich and who not. The fishermen and the workers at the Arsenal retained their faith in the efficacy of the churches and kept them steadily supplied with their offerings. Yet the storms on the Lagoon were not terrifying. So their very liberal donations were purely for the sake of kudos. There were no beggars; everyone begged, and, for introducing you to a glassblower, a marquis of the most ancient lineage inscribed in the Golden Register would get a commission and, if necessary, ask for it. This was happening in 1951 and the Golden Register was closed in 1370. I saw a working-class woman taking a piece of brocade to the sacristan of San Giorgio degli Schiavoni. In the course of the day the people with me showed me the shop where she had bought it. There was no mistake: we asked to see the material. It came from a very fine fifteenth-century ceremonial robe which they cut up with scissors. It was to decorate the statue of St. George to whom, for reasons unknown, ordinary people had a firm devotion, and nothing was too fine for him. The shopkeeper told us that in this way he made three times as much money as from selling the whole robe to a rich collector. It was not unusual to see offerings of fruit and bottles of wine instead of flowers made to saints when it wasn't their feast day. The beadles and priest let these tributes stand for at least a day at the foot of the statues. There was no politics—openly, anyway—and what was done clandestinely was so complicated that it wasn't politics any longer. But there were no laborers in the city, only craftsmen (so it was said), and if they were good at their work they thought themselves the equals of Rothschild, and happier into the bargain. That was the natural source of the universal generosity. Nothing counted except art for art's sake. They made people pay, of course, but they always preferred a nice gesture which ranked as money. Clearly it was not a question of morality, but in Venice evil often gave rise to good. At any rate, the more elevated social life there was based on the fact that pride, to a quite insane degree, came first, and this easily assuaged more misery than a truckload of democratic legislation. Among those for whom pride was so important, life was free and easy, as long as your nature allowed you to fall in step with them, and as long as you were inclined to humor. Their generosity was so subtly refined as to ensure that everything was arranged so that they never acted in earnest. They would be slain or slay to proclaim the preeminence of their sex, their position, their passion or art, which, in fact, they did not believe in. This lack of faith afforded the purest air that a man or woman could possibly breathe in 1951. It was so heady as to prompt them to acts of mad abandon. Which, indeed, they committed. This was the last area of the old Europe where that happened. There, to be sure, as everywhere, worthy rivals to Cromwell's horsemen were in evidence, but they were forced to follow the lead of the violins: the sight was comical. The last bastion was falling, but calmly, in broad daylight.

Since I am discussing customary behavior and passionate emotions, I must mention the little details that bear witness to them. On the pullovers worn by workers in the Arsenal, sailors and ordinary working men in general, I noticed a little pocket or, more exactly, a tiny case the size of an index finger and positioned quite low down. It also accompanied the two traditional waistcoat pockets among middle-class people, and I saw it on a windbreaker in the window of a high-class menswear shop. It was designed to hold a tiny lead figure of St. Antony of Padua, which they always had with them. The saint, who was three centimeters long, had to be carried vertically, at the level of the liver. All the specialist embroidery and knitting magazines, though only those published in Venice, took this custom into account. Women of every class had a St. Antony in their bags. He wasn't there to help them find things they had lost. It was a matter of the decisions you are always having to make in life. In the street you saw women suddenly pressing their bags against the position of their livers. They weren't plagued by stomachache or stitches in their sides. They were busy saying to St. Antony of Padua: "It's up to you now, little one!" They were no longer responsible for the sin they were about to commit. It was being ratified by a little lead guardian who was also a well-known saint. Much (very much!) less refined than Pascal, of course, but if happiness was at stake, much more effective—and *God hadn't been left out.*

I heard political talk, and from men at their ease, sunning themselves, because we had had several days of fairly intense cold. I had the impression that their outlook was sound, if by a sound outlook one means trust in humanity and a belief that human beings are infinitely capable of exhibiting moral qualities when faced with any test. To look at them, you would have supposed they were guests at Trimalchio's banquet in Petronius' *Satyricon*. When Venetian men were past forty and the way of things had inevitably lowered their sights, they were often very handsome creatures. They ran to a somewhat feminine, Neronic corpulence. They had ignored the Dalmatian wind and left their shirts open, revealing ample breasts covered in black hair. I stayed there for more than an hour, pretending to read a book, pleased to have encountered such charming Robespierres. Absolutely corrupt, they were still corruptible (like everyone else). They uttered not a single idiocy. Given the nature of the subject, that demanded an unusual understanding of things.

I watched a ceremonial gondola passing. Municipal workers were probably taking it for a refit. It was red, whereas ordinary gondolas were black (to commemorate a vow made during the plague). I had always wondered why, for example, Canaletto had not been able to give a festive note to the Doge's trip on the *Bucentoro* on a May morning. He had emphasized the gold and red, and here especially red was like a warning shot: it made people nervous. That black, however, was very soothing in the Venetian light. I have already said how pure it was because of the absence of any dust. It was also the only color that added something new to the intense clarity. In the long run other colors became tedious because they repeated what the sun had already said, which was quite enough to deal with anyway.

"The fact that I count on Providence proves that I believe in God." That was a very Venetian affirmation. In this city with three meters of water at every threshold, children were quite free to do whatever they wanted. You could see groups of them engaged in who knows what dark enterprise, and looking very serious about it. I was told that very few of them were drowned. Moreover, they considered themselves to possess all the passions of outstanding individuals and to be favored by destiny. They did not believe, as people did else-where, that it took twenty years to make a man, but that he became one just like that. I never saw any doting mothers. They treated their children like their husbands and men (and women) in general: as if they knew all there was to know about them. Consequently, hypocrisy was totally absent from all their enthusiasms, and you never had to suffer a fool gladly, whether male or female. This made the atmosphere in the streets very cheerful.

It was unwise to make several appointments on the same day. You had to move about by foot and in a labyrinth, or by gliding slowly along the waterways. A gondolier was not a taxi driver. He was often forced to put you down a hundred and fifty meters from the place where you were going and, as soon as you had touched ground, he lost all interest in you. There wasn't the least ill will about this; he just didn't know. The most serious aspect of this was that no one knew. If it was a matter of getting to a specific place, if you didn't know the way and particularly if you asked, and you had a hundred and fifty meters to go, it would take you a good hour. On arriving late somewhere you would be punished. The faces of the people waiting for you were so happy and contented that you had the distressing feeling that you were not late, but too late, and that you had missed the best thing. If you really liked the person in question, it was more than upsetting. Of course the happiness and contentment resulted from those who held you most dear having been asleep until your arrival. All this was soon apparent, but that, even relying on the most accom-modating sensitivity, did not put things right. It was a frequent source of misunderstandings that added a certain harshness to some Venetian afternoons. On the other hand, if you got there on time it was one of the rare places in the world where it was permissible to enjoy feelings between people openly. Friendship, for instance (on condition it had been sealed for some years), was a sacrament, and indissoluble. You could write a hundred tragedies entitled *Friends in Venice*. It was scarcely consonant with fashionable politics. I came across an activist from one or other party who was suffering horribly because he was determined to sacrifice everything to the need to be on time where his heart was.

There were no cars. You had constantly to remember this, especially when you saw such calm people. The owner of the latest model of the finest vehicle was altered beyond recognition after eight days of alleyways and canals, particularly if he or she had not decided to return to Autorimessa (where the glass garage seemed so safe and convenient that you could comfortably forget the favorite car you had parked there). People afflicted by the most appalling mannerisms became attractive. Fifteen days of walking about punctuated by restful trips in gondolas imbued your stance with an aristocratic nonchalance. Everything had to be done slowly, and soon the only sounds to impinge upon the ear were silky soft. There were no more sharp exchanges in conversation. This made it possible to see things straight, and not to be taken in by the suasions of the heart on more than one out of every two occasions. No one went flat out in any enterprise. This meant that even the indolent were not unresourceful and were able to defend their contentment with astonishing vigor.

We went to a concert in St. Mark's Square given by the Venice Municipal Orchestra. It was the most unrelieved cacophony ever. The musicians arrived one after the other, still doing up their uniforms. When a little man in charge decided that everyone he needed was there, without any more ado he raised his baton and the instruments began to emit their several wails. It was impossible to make anything specific of this noise. The square was packed with people, and I thought there was going to be a revolution. Not at all: everyone went on strolling about as if nothing was amiss. We were seated on the terrace of Florian's café, which was very crowded. I was near a pillar that concealed an enthusiast in the seventh heaven of pleasure. I have never observed a happier face. The signs of his enjoyment of the proceedings were so extreme that I can describe them only as obscenely immodest. So much so that I wondered if I too hadn't gone crazy. To reassure myself I had to find a program and search out the title of the piece they were playing. It was a very well-known work, which I knew so well that I could even hum it. This meant that the off-key bawling of the trombones and the ghastly unalloyed squawking of all the other instruments were not in fact an interpretation of some contemporary masterpiece with the usual informed admirers. It took some time before I began to see that the entire audience was performing and that they were engaged in a rendition of sensual pleasure. I am sure that my music lover liked Mozart. In the intervals he tipped his chair so that his face was obscured. He was resting between bouts of acting. When he reemerged into the light he did not immediately repress the very evident quivering of his sensitive mouth. In Venice people were heroes not "for the tsar and for Holy Russia" but for the gallery.

In the Merceria the other morning I had been surprised by the admiring looks I received. There had even been some very direct declarations of love. I wondered what was happening to me. It took me a very long time to work it out. In the end it turned out to be something that would have seemed quite laughable anywhere else. A couple of paces ahead of me a huge policeman in a bearskin hat and with a red plume was striding along very grandly, swinging his violet greatcoat. I had automatically fallen in step with him, and it looked as if he were my majordomo charged with the task of clearing the crowd for my progress. That's what they thought, and a very stylish old man saluted me. I let the joke last right up to the Banca d'Italia and then pretended to go in there. When I told the story, I was congratulated for this particular piece of cunning. It would have been impolite to have enlightened too abruptly people who, as I was reminded, *had played along with things*.

It was constantly necessary to resort to the most accomplished of civilized ploys: in other words, to deceit. Merely walking in step behind a policeman tricked up like that could have opened up a marvelous future for me. The annoying thing was that they also drew the wildest conclusions from mere silence and the absence of a policeman.

I needed a barber. I had found one in a little street. Since I paid the assistant with a thousand-lire note and he had to give me the change, the owner said out loud, though in dialect: "Give him the wrong note." This was a five-hundred-lire note which, naturally, I rejected. "He saw through it," said the assistant, who immediately became very nice and brushed me down vigorously from top to bottom until he was almost on his knees. A hundred little tricks of this kind were played throughout every day but always had some appealing side to them. There was the bar which charged more inside than on the terrace because it was cool inside, so the waiter said. In the winter you had to pay more on the terrace because it was sunny there. I had some fun bargaining for obscene photographs. There were some at fifty and others at a hundred lire. I asked why: they were the same. She tried to prove that the hundred-lire shots showed some detail more in focus. There were yet others at a thousand lire which were just as ugly as the rest. They cost more, it seemed, because the protagonists had "put more of their heart into it." That is exactly what she said. The person who spoke about the "heart" in this way was an old woman whose breasts must have weighed at least thirty kilos and who tried to flirt with me. In Venice, it seemed, these Towers of Babel had more admirers that one would ever have believed possible. In places generously endowed with it, beauty grows wearisome. I saw many very beautiful women there. They told me that eighty percent of them were stupid. I did not believe this, in view of the abilities they had to summon up every minute of the day merely to defend themselves. They assured me that these women were devoid of talent. That was why you saw so many discontented men always looking for a brilliant woman. They narrated a hundred tales of occasions which ended up as desultory conversations because the real thing was such a rarity. These were people all but exploding with imagination that just had to find an outlet. This was a much more demanding requirement. After all, they could have the other whenever they wanted it on any street corner. This was the source of that triumphal virility which the men there affected. You had always to remember that they were quite capable of bursting into tears at the least vexation. I seem to be criticizing them, but I am merely trying to see things plainly. It was all a matter of latitude and of the clarity of the air. It was a region without illusions. Reality was soon perceived for what it was. Then they grew bored, and any distraction would do if tedium threatened.

Yet I had already seen the light of Venice somewhere else: in the far north of Scotland, on the Atlantic coast, near

Mallaig. There, too, the lack of trees and the vast echoing stretches of water made the daylight so white that no particular colors could be discerned as such. There, too, the mist-wrapped expanses of darkness were lusciously, purely black. But the Sutherland Scots satisfied their needs in other ways. Since reality afforded them no basic elements to work with they imported fragments of an unreal world. Ghostly shapes walked the moors of Rannoch, and at Fort William, Glencoe, Nairn, and Cawdor. There it was a question not of seduction but of being haunted. But this derived from the same demands. A hundred times already, on the Fondamenta Nuove, at San-Pietro di Castello, at San-Spirito de Padre Francescani, or merely on the Riva degli Schiavoni, I had imagined I was actually on the road to the Isles, between Lochinvar and Lairg. It was the same light, the same mixture of white and black, and the same sun squandered here and diluted there. All the Venetians needed to persuade them to create ghosts was deprivation.

We went to the Lido like everyone else. It was a beach like any other. It happened to be heavy weather. That enabled us to avoid the pedal craft and the pemmican drying on the sand. The Adriatic was bounding. The little wooden huts where they sold coffee, lemonade, and sandwiches were deserted. The angry wind made their thin partition walls shudder. The foam and great packages of green water attacked their thresholds. A few big birds like those you found in the mountains tried in vain to get back to Albania. Used as I was to scorching Mediterranean horizons, I was amazed to discover how cold the far reaches of the Adriatic were. It was that which made me think of Scotland; and also the way in which the high waves rolled in, which was so different from the breaking of the Mediterranean storms on the rocks. Only

Elise and I were there. She was often forced to shelter behind fences until the strongest gusts were over. Quite alone on this Lungomare with its raging foam, we understood the need for lies or departure. On reflection I found the concert given by the municipal orchestra quite appropriate, and I was not so far from rehearsing on my own features the automatic bliss of the music lover at Florian's the other evening. The buildings and the trees on the Lido island were recent. In the first place there had probably been only an almost bare seafront on the side of the Lagoon. At Venice, from the banks of St. Mark's canal over the Lido walls, scarcely higher than the sand, it must have been possible to see the Adriatic storms and this rising, tumultuous tide that led to Constantinople. The Venetian Republic can have remained *serenissima*, so serene, for so long only because it did not play the reality game like Florence. For every hundred Venetians who left for Asia, twenty thousand had stayed who were forced to dissemble incessantly. Without such consolations, the people would have abandoned themselves to every extremity of despair in this half-submerged city around which nothing towered.

Venice, indeed, was a place where you tasted palpable reality. There were too many boats to allow the manufacture of characters capable of vanquishing death. The flat water, the whiteness of the light, the silence, and the slow pace at which everyone was compelled to move confirmed the existence of a beyond where no midnight pass would be accepted. Instead they fell back on what actually existed. The constant use they made of their reality stimulated their faculty for draining its pleasures to the very last drop.

The shops in Venice were stocked with the most extraordinary things. You could buy false mustaches, little steel hoops that supported your arches and prevented flat feet, trusses, flannel bandages, scented matches, stuff that made shoes creak, another that made ties soft, padded jackets that enabled you to throw out your chest without effort, gossamer-light nylon stockings to make your sandaled feet sun-bronzed, and unconvincing black cloth teeth. I knew a very pretty woman who often made use of this last device to pretend she was gap-toothed and get some peace when she was out. They told me that some handsome men did the same. In a little street near San-Giorgio degli Schiavoni they sold a kind of wallet which anywhere else would have seemed a trick but was taken very seriously here: it was an artificially swollen wallet fringed with the edges of a wad of stage money. This was known as a *colosseo* (a meaningless word). They pointed out how easy it was to carry this *colosseo,* so light that it was no problem at all in a shirt or trouser pocket in even the most trying heat. Of course everyone saw through it, as was obvious. No one was *completely* taken in. Nevertheless, it seemed that these *colosseos* worked wonders in a great number of cases. When I suggested that using them must cause some problems, they reminded me of the gentle air and the light on the sand which so satisfied your senses that you were predisposed to be forgiving.

Nothing was so suitable as an end-of-autumn evening, when summer appetites had been sated, and a wind from Hungary disturbed the surface of the Lagoon, for a stroll at the edge of these shallow waters opened up by the swell to the very silt below. Assuredly Venice was the only place in the world where you could renew your wishes indefinitely. If you wish to keep only to coarse historical fact, the site for the city was chosen by people who wished to be able to defend themselves easily. But I think they wanted to be under constant attack. In Venice the sea gave off that strong smell which emanates from all victories and makes them desirable. I find statistics unhelpful. At the risk of upsetting romantic spirits, I am forced to state that there are no suicides in Venice. Those who make for the city with that intention should take their lives the night they get there; the next day will be too late. As for born Venetians, they are concerned only with a hundred thousand ways of living. I admire people who rely on historical reality, the stuff of which is impalpable and wholly unconnected with emirical reality. The Venetians are enthusiasts in search of temptations and chose this spot so that they could yield to them continually. That was the source of their most serene Republic, and their laws.

One afternoon I got the time wrong. I arrived at the Accademia when the doors were already shut. While waiting for them to open again, we went for a walk, Elise and I, around San-Trovaso. We made our way along the side of a very sunny canal until we came to a big empty square. In front of a ruined church, assailed by laurels growing through its stone walls, some old corn-threshing cylinders had been abandoned in thick grass at the foot of an old mulberry tree. Through a gap between two rows of houses with closed shutters, we watched a lone sailing barge with a cargo of marble blocks pass slowly, noiselessly, along the Canal della Giudecca.

We often had this feeling that the things we saw were glimpsed in dreams. If, however, you are afraid that sights of this kind will not be vouchsafed you when alone (though any sensitive person must succeed in this quite happily after a day or two of freedom from restraint), then you must take as your guide one of those sad yet calm children whose play consists of a close examination of their toes on the quays of the Dogana di Mare. The child will certainly take you at once to the Grand Canal, St. Mark's Square, or the Riva degli

Schiavoni. Then all you have to do is to buy from any shop one of those whistles made from bored-through apricot-stones that you twirl at the end of a string, and that so perfectly imitate the mournful mewing of a gull. Your guide will immediately understand what is required. However lacking you are in communicative ability, and though you tell him in ever so few words, he will take you where you want to go.

But I must agree with bigots of all persuasions: Venice is a haunt of perdition where no devotee can trust another. Statistics will bear me out yet again. The extreme political parties were poorly represented there. Admittedly they had a certain number of members, but, after all, Venice is in Italy and Italy is cautious. Since it was wise to back all the runners, everyone *also* laid a bet on at least one of the radical parties. "You never know" was the appropriate catchphrase. In Venice, a latter-day Robespierre would never have found a carpenter prepared to make him a stand strong enough to sustain the action of a guillotine. The carpenter would have made sure he was busy at something else. The same was true of religion. The church bells rang and even sounded very fine. The clergy busied themselves appropriately around pulpits, shrines, and altars, but some of their number were never to be seen carrying sacred objects; their faces bore the marks of the most congenial refinement: they were the accountants.

As for sin, there were masks everywhere, or, more precisely, half-masks or eye masks. This very attractive device, made from taffeta, velvet, or silk, disguised the forehead, eyes, and nose, and left the mouth uncovered. The look directed from the midst of such a dark, impassive half-countenance came straight from the Golden Age. I tried on some of these masks to see how they changed my state of mind. I do not wish to say exactly what they did to me. But when I looked in the mirror I saw that an eye mask made me a more difficult prey to seize and that even my hearty laughter had become an ambiguous smile. What a splendid ploy in the present-day world! The good thing about it was that you could wear a mask out of doors at any time without causing scandal. They would merely commiserate with you.

I was told the following story. In 1846 a young man arrived in Venice whose passport said that he belonged to the Lanza family of Turin. In Venice, which was then under firm Austrian control, it was very acceptable socially to have a name that often appeared as the byline to articles against the Italian nationalist politician Mazzini. The young man was very elegant and behaved "exactly as the rich would do." He had black hair and very neat muttonchop whiskers, and a face totally lacking in arrogance. He had clearly come to spend his time with women, and the best-looking of them burst out laughing when they discovered that the police had dispatched a mounted agent to the Lanzas to get the lowdown. "But we already know it," said the ladies. "All you have to do is to look at the suspect's face to see that he has a Lanza nose." "We are quite well aware of his nose," said the police, who had a few pretty women in their pocket anyway, "but we want to know if it is worth risking several florins on this young man when he's cleaned out. And that moment isn't far off if he gives two or three more parties like that one the other night, which was well above the level of what even the Lanzas can afford. We need some discreet information about what's happening in the monarchical party in Piedmont, and the right moment will certainly come when this young fellow will be very pleased to sing for his supper. We want to know if he knows anything worth finding out." Well, clearly the police said a great deal, and when they have a great deal to say they might even have a real idea in their heads.

This was the time of the Mazzini oaths. In Liguria, Lombardy, and Piedmont, there were more secret societies than grocers' shops: Young Italy, the Good Cousins, the Federati, the Sanfedists, the Hetairi. They had never assassinated any monarch but they had been foolish enough to say out loud every night that they would do so one of these days. And the nights in Italy are very clear. It was sufficient to have a copy of a Genoa paper in your pocket to be sentenced to death. Every weekend, King Charles Albert of Sardinia lent his hangman to Milan. In Venice, the Austrians were better organized and had three executioners at work every single day.

The day after the mounted officer left, one of the young man's inamoratas who was more responsive than the others to his attentions said: "Giacomo, I don't want to lose you." On occasions like this it is very difficult to conceal the truth. If this young woman—Ermelinda, one of the actresses at La Fenice—still had any doubts, they were removed by her partner's immediate perception of all that she half-conveyed. But she was overwhelmed by the fact that he was still looking at her tenderly. She was used to appearing very early every day in the secret office of a prefect of police who intensely disliked the dawn and women, and whose only interest was the maintenance of order. "The man they've sent," she continued, "is called Barbieri, and he has gone to see your king with a *biglietto privelegiato*. But there is something that no one knows, except those in charge, and me: for two weeks Barbieri has been making love to a young woman from the Fondato dei Turchi." And, after a short silence: "She is a brunette, and I must humbly admit that she's a hundred times better than I am. But I am going to tell you her name, which is Rosa Pesaro; and she has a room behind the Palazzo Grimani in the only house with an iron lantern. I know that Barbieri is very jealous. He is still possessed by the first flush of passion, as I told you, and after four days away he will certainly stop off at the lantern before going on to the prefecture of police." "I am afraid of nothing," said Giacomo, "but if I were, I would find it a simple matter to keep at least a hundred paces away from this Rosa Pesaro. I detest the smell of fish, and she could not be possibly be worth even one of you. I know the house with the lantern very well. You can only get to it by boat and from the Foscari Canal. People like Barbieri always think that it is very clever to arrive from Mestre in the middle of the night." "You don't trust me," said Ermelinda, her eyes now full of tears, "but if what you're thinking of is what you really want to do [at this he stroked her hair, which was very lovely indeed], promise me not to rely on the cleverness you speak of. They offer a very substantial bonus for every execution; it can be as much as a florin. That will make Barbieri very sharp indeed."

Of course the horseman did not return. They dispatched another. When the third was sent, Ermelinda said, "I'm afraid." "We've nothing to worry about," said Giacomo. "Fifty women—of whom you are one—will steadfastly testify to all my actions, and swear an oath to that effect on the Holy Sacrament. Even," he added, "people who don't like me very much or, rather, who don't like me at all and yet would recoil at the thought of committing a mortal sin." "That is why," said Ermelinda, "I'm doubly afraid. Above all of the prefect, whose anger at being hoaxed will eventually overcome his discretion and take due effect; but also of you, for you are the devil incarnate." Giacomo was very handsome when he began to laugh. "You and your Italy—how stupid you are," said Ermelinda. "You must be unaware that the firing squad will aim at your face with nicked bullets if there's no mother, wife, or woman like me to tip them in advance. And I'm very poor."

This last statement, *her actual words*, was irresistible.

The Austrian chief of police was no fool. He simulated the anger expected of him. He meticulously set about preparing an arrangement that would allow him to save the situation without losing face. Until more reliable information was available, the man in question seemed to be a Lanza, and the Lanzas were the supporters of Throne and Altar. This was no business that you could bring to an abrupt end by resorting to the gallows or the *cavaletti* (benches on which the victim was laid before being beaten with rods). Barbieri and the two other mounted policemen were declared "transferred to the service of the Kingdom of Sardinia." The best society of Venice unanimously applauded this charming euphemism. Finally, the secretary general of the prefecture himself departed with an armed and suitably equipped company, ostensibly for Turin.

"Don't worry, my little pigeon," said Ermelinda, as happy as could be, "women are less egotistical than men. My happiness is not restricted to the hours I spend with you in this little bedroom. I am constantly engaged in trying to preserve this beloved and most mysterious head, which, at this very moment, I see, is thinking of Italy or possibly even—which would be much more serious—of another woman. But yes, you are right: I belong to you, so let me know that I am enslaved. For you I have listened at doors. This is what I suggest. Have a handsome red platform put in your gondola and tomorrow we shall spend the day at Torcello. I very much want to see the mosaics in the cathedral, and I shall show you something that you will enjoy immensely. Have a decent meal made ready here with champagne, and we shall eat it when we return. We shall certainly be ready for it."

"I seem mysterious only because I have nothing to say," Giacomo replied. "In fact, I immediately told everyone, you included, the truth. Woe betide me when you eventually realize what is as clear as daylight: that is, that I am just a true Lanza, as I have constantly told you. Do you know what I think will happen? All at once, I shall lose the glory that this imagined conspirator has assumed in your eyes, and you will send me back to my beloved books. So I intend to profit from your supposition while there is still time. The red-draped gondola will be before your door at ten o'clock tomorrow morning. Is that early enough?"

"It's early enough to leave," said Ermelinda sweetly, "but come at seven. The gondola will wait. The red has a purpose. I want to send someone into a perfect rage. However enjoyable that may prove to be, the best time will come when we are together tomorrow evening. Don't forget the champagne."

Torcello is a kilometer to the north of Burano. It is a little village of deep solitude, for even now it retains traces of the Lagoon's earliest civilization. There is a vast Byzantine mosaic of the Last Judgment inside the cathedral there.

"Come along," said Ermelinda as soon as they had disembarked, "and be as quiet as a mouse. This will certainly amuse you. I just cannot wait any longer." She led him through deserted alleyways to a little house at the water's edge. There, concealed behind a little hedge of willow, they saw the secretary general of the prefecture in shirt sleeves, fishing very peacefully with his rod and line. The policemen with all accoutrements laid aside and the maids out of uniform were taking their siesta in the grass, under a willow tree.

"Now we shall go back to Burano, and then to Venice," said Ermelinda. "I wanted you to see that all danger for us is past. Now there will be no need for you to put opium in my tisane. The really quaint thing is that they are here by order. When they return, you will be a Lanza as your passport says, and the prefect will be able to smile if ever he meets you. Don't say a word. Look how lovely the sun is. When the third policeman, the big one with those long yellow mustaches, was transferred to the service of the Kingdom of Sardinia, I watched you count the drops into my cup. The very great care you took with your little spoon to make sure that the dose wasn't too severe went straight to my heart. I decided that you might even feel something for me."

Some time afterward, when Giacomo was returning from a game of bowls on the Piazza d'Armi, and was crossing through the alleys of the Secco Marina, he noticed a beautiful brunette who could have been the model for a symbol of the people on a coin. She seemed to be waiting for someone. It was Rosa Pesaro. She was young and very full-blooded; she missed Barbieri, who had been as robust as she could have wished. As Giacomo came level with her, she shouted out the vilest accusations, above all that he had "killed to stay alive." In that heavily populated area staying alive meant eating. Very soon ten or so of those tough laborers from the Arsenal appeared on the street, and about twelve of the kind of women worth several men when they exploded. Giacomo's face was soon clawed, and blood streamed from him. Rosa had deftly torn his shirt and then, of course, enraged by this ridiculous onslaught, he tried to get in some blows himself. This was quite ineffective. Finally, he was stupid enough to call out to these creatures who went entirely by how things looked; he used words and statements that they could not understand, and that had to do with freedom, and more exactly *their* freedom. In the end he was clubbed and hacked to pieces with iron chairs that they had fetched from the terrace of a little café.

I am particularly interested, as must be apparent, in stories that depict the course of emotions from 1830 to 1850, and above all in political passions. The character whom I called Angelo in *The Horseman on the Roof* had not only experienced the cholera of 1831. On this side of the Alps, too (if not in the Venice region, which had remained Austrian after 1848, then at least in Lombardy and Piedmont), he had had adventures that I wanted to describe.

This tale of Giacomo I heard from a very sensitive woman whose purity was above suspicion, but under the title of *The Story of Ermelinda*. When I happened to remark ingenuously that I thought it should really be the story of Giacomo, she observed, with an infinitesimal disdain that only three hundred years of lofty cultural heritage could justify, that it was truly amazing to find me missing the point so ineptly. The intention, it seemed, had been that I should admire the consummate skill with which Ermelinda had managed the whole affair, without losing her victim's trust for a single instant, and while enjoying the most human of pleasures with someone who, though his ideas were execrable, was certainly lovable.

Venetians from the oldest top drawer were melancholy by nature. They liked fine cloth, superb jewellry, and exquisite perfumes. They wore the kind of suits that Apollo and Jupiter would wear in 1952. They appreciated good food but exercised the moderation that adds a special refinement to sinning. They had considerable taste and their taste was good.

Both men and women had delicately jointed limbs. They knew how to walk. They walked only in the evening, on St. Mark's Square, but with the same elegant reserve with which people of their standing would dance. They said little and constantly acknowledged the grace of Providence. This was true even of women who were being wooed. The fact was, they could "see the unhappy side of things," and spy misfortune in advance. For them, everything was a source of anxiety, for they interpreted everything. If you found a cool little breeze rather nice, they would shiver and predict the bitter cold to come. If the weather was good, it was *too* good. If the good weather lasted, this good weather could not last. It is easy to imagine what people of this disposition would make of any passion once within its ineluctable grasp. And grasped by passions they were. I don't mean just love but ambition, for instance, or a passion for collecting intaglios. Then, of course, there was avarice, which produced extraordinary results, and pride. All this made you subject to an all-enveloping (and grim) pathos. There were times when you were in a tight corner. You thought you were simply eating and wiping your mouth; but not at all: suddenly there were a thousand Cassandras after you. There are many anecdotes in this respect that I shall (probably) not relate, for the events they refer to are recent, and what and whom they concern will be obvious. As soon as you put your foot inside a hallway when you were merely on your way to have tea with someone, you were liable to hear: "Alas! Oh, most mournful. Alas, alack!— Apollo's angry; and the heavens themselves do strike. . . ." And nine times out ten their fears were justified. They guessed right. It was very distressing if you were not a Venetian. All the more so because, apart from this, they were delightful people, and desirable in every sense of the word. But you were reluctant to press things when their pack included the master card of imminent bad luck. Only Don Juan himself (who really belonged here more than in Spain) could have coped with the situation. I should more than like to tell all that I learned. It may be summarized by saying that it was not enough to win; you had to relish the experience of winning. Religious or moral scruples played no part in this agonizing drama. This made the odds relentless. The choice was not good or evil but evil or nothing. You were offered vast riches but at the price of unparalleled misfortune. That was the rule of the game. Unhappiness was not a punishment but the issue of crime. It was normal currency and taken for granted. When I realized this was the prevailing attitude, I too made sure that I behaved acceptably where acceptance mattered. These circles included a considerable number of nuns who were between twenty-five and thirty years of age and very beautiful. You met them in drawing rooms. There they behaved like anyone else, and their approach to things was just as melancholy. I saw some of them dancing with one another, and not innocent polkas but dances so up to date that I don't know what they were called, but they amounted to a kind of slow, ecstatic saunter. It was sinister. I always prepared for the growling thunder that would surely shake the palace. They expected it too, as did the charming young man playing the piano with amazing brio. There was no remedy for his doom-laden anguish, to counter which, in the end, it was obvious all things were permitted; it was hereditary and born in the blood. To trace its origins, you would have to go all the way back to those Venetians who entrusted all their fortunes to the sea and spent their time pacing up and down the quays, their minds tossing on the ocean and ready to interpret the least whisper of the wind. Shakespeare portrays this admirably in the first scene of *The Merchant of Venice*.

Yet all those without pretensions to higher social status (among whom you could make real friends) were marvelously endowed for a happy life. I tried to find out how far they trusted the political party that promised it to them, at the price of a change in the status quo. They were like chickens who have come across a knife. They joined one passion to another until they managed to enjoy, and enjoy fiercely, what we would find boring. For them the seven deadly sins were like the different tastes in a mixed ice cream, where you get, say, coffee and vanilla at one and the same time. There was too much, indeed a universal, emphasis on general happiness, not so much because, like everyone else, they were all for it, but because they approached the idea as they did everything: with the resolute intention of *immediately* getting some source of pleasure out of it in one way or another. They succeeded very well in this. They realized that it gave them something they could use to flavor so-called serious conversations and lift themselves above the ordinary run. You had to get them going on this subject and to let them talk: you could learn a lot in this way. Above all, once they had spoken their minds, you had to remain with them and to see them living, if only for a week. Then you began to appreciate their philosophy of life. I don't mean by this that they were inoffensive. The search for happiness (especially if you are as gifted as they were for the venture) is no philanthropic enterprise. But they were no more dangerous than people of any era. There was no modern danger in Venice. They lied only for the sake of personal advantage. They never committed a crime for the sake of an idea: merely crimes of special interest, simple, straightforward, and precise. They were sharp enough to despise the common good. This was also a product of their city or, rather, of the city as it was, for they had made it what it was.

I knew of some ten little private industries in Venice. You mustn't think that life there consisted mainly of fancy-dress balls, trips in gondolas, film festivals, and all the fun of Sodom and Gomorrah. Apart from the above-mentioned minor industries, there were plenty of artisans, all the way from carpenters, shoemakers, and tailors to the funereal ornamentalists who made the decorations for graves (some of these ornaments were as beautiful as Mexican idols), rope-makers, and so on. It was also one of these few cities where blacksmiths and farriers were still to be found. I wondered what they might still be called on to shoe, but in fact blacksmiths and farriers had forges that opened onto the street, or rather onto the alley, along a *canaletto* ringing with the noise of the anvil. All this little world was alive and enjoyed daily celebrations unknown to the newspapers. There were fishing parties, family meals, siestas, plots, meetings, pipes smoked out in the open. All this proceeded without interruption, as in the great age when there were no tourists, and people went to Venice as to Romorantin.

Tourists had made this city a backdrop for tourist activities. There was a touch of Ruskin, and Wagner, and D'Annunzio, and Mussolini, and now Laurel and Hardy, about it. If you were unaware that it was a city mainly for the use of Venetians, you saw scarcely anything of the real Venice. I visited the museums, as everyone did, and I went for a trip in a gondola on the Grand Canal. I soon tired of that. You came across similarly engaged Germans, English, French, Chinese, Turks (but no Spaniards). Their heads were mounted on pivots: they looked here, there, and everywhere, as if time was everything (and for them, indeed, it was). If I want to be happy, I have to be sure that I am among people whose faces plainly declare that there will be a tomorrow. I go about everything slowly. That is what I like. If people are in a rush, whatever the reason, I leave to avoid catching whatever has infected them. So, if they told me, with their eyes popping out of their heads, that I *just had to* see this or that, I would probably go for a siesta with a detective novel. I wandered about, to be sure, with a guidebook in my hand. I did not go around like one of those self-important idiots who want to be taken for locals. I have many other faults, but not that. So, quite openly, I carried the breviary proper to a childish, self-declared tourist. Anyway, it came in useful for streetcar tickets (*vaporetti* tickets, in Venice). Then there were postcards, especially the misleading ones. That was what I wanted. And that is why I have not mentioned the Rezzonico Palace, the Rialto Bridge, the Vendramin-Calergi Palace, and the Ca d'Oro. I saw them, of course, but in addition to other things. Yet I also entered, in humble amazement, tens of extraordinary houses like the house I lived in at Manosque with my father and mother throughout my youth. Elise and I (I went first, of course) ascended staircases leading to sordid and magnificent apartments we had dreamed of when we were sixteen. On landings piled with slop pails and baskets of vegetables, I chatted with housewives fighting to survive on fixed budgets. Like everyone there, they made a mutton stew on Thursday, and a beef stew on Sunday, and on Mondays ate the leftovers as a hash with onions. Their little boys went, as I did, to the grocer's for two hundred grams of grated cheese; the only difference was that my portion cost at most ten centimes.

In certain streets, behind the Palazzo Trevisano, toward the Piazza Manini or San-Giovanni Chrisostomo, you had to go by water. The houses were set in water two or three meters deep at the thresholds. However poor you were, you had to have your own boat, and a little private harbor in the corridor. It didn't matter whether you were a carpenter, cobbler, or tailor, you also had to be a boatman and make your way to your customers like Charon ferrying the dead across the rivers of the Underworld. That changes many things. Even if she had to haggle over the shoulder of mutton, a housewife would single-scull her boat quite uncomplainingly to do her shopping. She sat there in her "wherry," and did not trail along the pavement with a string bag hanging from her arm. Her stream of consciousness just drifted. That was why these women had such proud features, and calm, even somewhat haughty, faces. They were used to calling out: a fine, raw cry to warn people they were coming as they turned the corners of the canal. Some of them, even quite young ones, would afford the luxury of poling their boats. They had considerable presence, as they stood there on the gunwales. The exercise of propelling the boats made their bodies long and supple, and them adroit enough to wear very wide petticoats and skirts that fell then tightened about their thighs in folds as impressive as the flutes of stone pillars. I noticed that they knew how to match the color of their skirts and blouses to the oily green of the water over which they glided, and to the reddish-brown of the walls roundabout. I was told that I was exaggerating and that it was sheer chance. I can accept that they chose the color without thinking about it, if that is what is meant, but then they must have been in that state of grace in which you live so freely that you need never be bored, for you are happy in and with everything you do.

V

Padua, Bologna, the Apennines

At Padua there was Giotto, and it was a joy to see him. Of course, like most people (who refuse to acknowledge it), I understand nothing about painting (as will become clear). I look for the feelings it may evoke. In this case, apprehension is not a stable instrument, like the intellect, but a variously contingent mechanism. It depends whether it is hot, or cold; whether everything is all right and I am in a good mood; or things are not up to the mark and I am worried about something. Sometimes a quite atrocious picture will give me immense pleasure, whereas I cannot see what is so very good in a superb painting. For instance, I like a harmony of blue and green just as you might like cauliflower or asparagus. If I find this consonance in a painter like Tartempion, and the moment is ripe, I am satisfied.

I experienced the same pleasure before the walls of the Scrovegni chapel in Padua that I had sometimes felt in front of a fine aquarium. Here the colors were at rest, but their interplay was the same as if they were mobile and immersed. I am thinking especially of the angel who appeared to Saint Anne and who is shown in the act of diving through the gable window toward a coral reef consisting of a chest and the tunicled figure of Anne surmounted by a halo. For me, the vision of Saint Joachim with its barren rocks also has something liquid about it, and perhaps this too is because of the angel who emerges from the blue sky like a tuna fish from the sea. As far as *Christ's Entry to Jerusalem* is concerned, it is entirely a matter of the colors: the whole group following Christ has exactly the same color as the fins of a goldfish breathing, and the marvelous rendering of the other group, to which Christ is drawing near, reminds me of the scales of salmon trout. One face, however (there are certainly a hundred others), that of the man (though I am not sure of that, for he looks some- what androgynous) in red, to the left of *The Marriage of the Virgin*, has nothing to do with the sea and the mysteries of the ocean, but only with the earth. This face is definitely of the here and now. But I have forgotten the sky in *Joseph Returning from the Temple*. It is precisely the same sky that I saw overhead in Piedmont at the beginning of my visit to Italy.

I had to see the Café Pedrocchi. I was quite impatient at the thought. It was still exactly as in the photograph of it at the front of volume 5 of Stendhal's *Journal* in the Champion edition. I was not at all anxious to drink the café's famous mocha coffee or to try one of its famous ices. All I wanted to do was to pass by slowly, without stopping. I wanted to see the terrace where Henri Beyle had so much bad luck, but I also wanted to lose sight of it straightaway, so that all its romantic qualities would stay with me forever.

And that was what I did. I enjoyed a few moments of quite intense happiness. This is tantamount to saying that art is not always everything. We all hunt in our own preserves.

I remembered one afternoon in Edinburgh. I had gone into some gallery or other while waiting for Aline, who was visiting the house where Burns stayed when he was in the city. What I really wanted to do was to sit down. I found only vast, totally deserted rooms hung with the portraits of historic figures. With very few exceptions, they were extremely mediocre paintings. There were Bonnie Prince Charlies and Flora MacDonalds galore, but a sharp little girl smiled at me from one gold frame as thick and heavy as the collar of a dray horse's harness. Later on, for me (but for me alone), this smile cast its magic over the whole of Scotland. I saw it everywhere, and it transformed everything with its enchantment.

Padua was a city ripe for intrigue. Whenever an average sensual Venetian had something going he went to Padua. In the good old days you went there slowly, in a boat and along a canal. But now you scorched off there at top speed on the highway. You were there in half an hour. You no longer had time to become a Paduan. That was why all those streets were full of visibly ill-prepared people.

In the square in front of the basilica they were still selling wax candles, as they always will be. They were a basic means of granting wishes, which, to be sure, know no bounds. The Piazza del Santo looked like the stage version of a North African desert. It was vast, sandy, sunlit, and windy—with the torrid groaning wind of the Underworld. You had to see the square in the crude, cruelly relentless sunlight of about two in the afternoon. The women selling candles were crouching in the shade of the low walls and sprang up from the ground as soon as they heard your footsteps. These housewives and mothers had all assumed the most pious of attitudes. It was amusing to watch and hear them tender their wares and try to arouse your most secret desires. I had never seen faces more replete with devotion yet at the same time so horribly, universally knowing. They forced you to blush at your innermost motives by offering you, as they said, "the means to get where you want."

In the background of the stage set were the Basilica of San Antonio, the Oratory of San Giorgio, and the Scuola, the raw and naked scenery of this inward conflict.

I wandered over the Prato della Valle. It was an open space on the way out of the city, in the direction of Mantua. In the middle of it they had planted a circle of very high trees on a round meadow. It had great charm, in spite of the three dozen statues gesticulating in three dozen ways. I walked over the stones leading to the series of facades in front of the Loggia Amulia. I was sure that if I lived in Padua this was where I would want to be. Everything there was full of character. Everywhere my thoughts were aroused and satisfied by minor pleasures seemingly dreamed up for me alone. I had already enjoyed this immensely sensual experience in Brescia. Here again, there was something that told me that art was not absolutely necessary, for me anyway. I had been happy thousands of times in my life. In order to be happy yet again in quite new ways (for I had changed with the years), all I needed was to rediscover that special harmony that had made me so very happy on this or that occasion already. Beauty did not automatically fill me with delight. Nothing, in fact, could make me happy, but anything could prompt me to become happy. Accordingly, I was always in a state of hope, and my heart was youthful and expectant. The sour and cynical take no nourishment and soon grow old. I love beauty, and of course it is in the realm of beauty that I search for whatever is before me, but I have to acknowledge that ugliness or—an even more strange and terrible admission— vulgarity sometimes succeeds where beauty fails.

I do not think I am the only person like this, and only the irredeemably naive would try to convince me of the contrary.

Life is not modeled from Carrara marble. There was nothing extraordinary on the Prato della Valle, but for me at five in the afternoon that day its light, atmosphere, sounds, colors, and shapes made me immeasurably happy. Yet I was the only one vouchsafed that strange, unique experience. Why should I not admit it?

I walked about here and there while waiting for my friend Paolo Pardi (I had named the Hussar in my novel after him). Signor Pardi had written an amazing book about the Italian Revolution of 1838. He had covered everyone and everything to do with it. Historical events are not devoted exclusively to monarchs. This must sound as if I wanted to stand up for the "infantry" in all walks of life, but you and I are neither kings nor geniuses, and we are always forgotten: no one ever pays any attention to the part we actually play in history. We never speak in beautifully chiseled sentences. At best we utter a confused array of purely private concerns studded with what are little better than expletives. Yet in the end, I believe, we say more than any Cambronne at Waterloo, with his "The Guards die, but do not surrender!"

During the French Revolution they changed the name of the Port-Royal to the "Port Libre"— the gate of freedom—and made a prison out of it. I find it immensely interesting to speculate how such things could ever have happened.

Like my entire generation, I had lived through a vast number of historical events since 1914. I had experienced them all from the viewpoint of someone living in Manosque, and in the quarter where I lived at that. For example, like everyone of my year of birth, I was called up in January 1915, but from August 1914 to January 1915 I discovered that the postman, not Field Marshal Joffre, was by far the most important person for all the people in our street. Who but Félicien Chabrier, the postman, according to whether he had a letter for you or not, could tell you whether Dieuze or the Marne was a victory or a defeat? In the same way, God had deserted both the church and the beyond, only to materialize in the form of a short, bald, and very bored secretary from the town hall, who went from door to door handing out the announcements about those killed in action. That is precisely the kind of history that scholars discard as "unimportant" and that I consider not just important but the only real history.

I was talking recently to a woman who was an old friend of my mother's. When we were still living at No. 14 in the Grande-Rue, Madame H. had a butcher's shop at No. 12. So the two shops were next door to one another. Madame H., who was ninety-two the other day, lost her only son at Verdun. I realized that for her the Second World War had never happened. For her, it had no historical reality whatsoever, and when I insisted that it did she said: "1939—that was nothing at all."

But my friend Pardi had written the ordinary, real history of the Revolution in Piedmont, Lombardy, Venice, and the Romagna. This is a period about which we in France know very little indeed, and it would be a great shame if we were to find something out about it only from the works of a traditional historian, irrespective of whether he is for or against revolutions. Pardi was neither for nor against them. The Revolution as such was of no interest to him, and this was the most convincing reason for crediting him with total impartiality. He was interested in the to-and-fro of human passions. He had developed an unusual method of studying this process. He made a list of all the villages, all the hamlets, all the farms, and all the mere crossings or clearings where there was the meanest woodcutter's or hunter's cabin. Then he got hold of the most detailed possible maps and found the locations of all the roads, paths, and tracks connecting all these centers of human life with one another. Day in, day out, for more than thirty years he walked along all these main and subsidiary arteries, and all these veins and veinlets, in which the rebellious blood of humankind ran and boiled. He ransacked the archives of police stations, courts, and lawyers' offices; he collected newspaper cuttings, interrogated old men and women, listened to bitter complaints, counted the dead and the heroes, reunited families, examined their traditions and memories, made an inventory of each heritage, and set his researcher's stethoscope to the briefcases of the past in order to listen to the breathing so characteristic of all revolutions; and then quite simply wrote down all these clinical observations one after the other. This was a long way from the bombast and melodrama of Mazzini. Yet Mazzini with his grandiose perorations was concerned with precisely the same "struggles for freedom and justice" over the reality of which my friend had labored so meticulously.

There had been a lot of killing then. They had killed the Austrians and the supporters of Austria. Perceptive individuals soon realized that it was advantageous to single out as supporters of Austria anyone they owed money to, anyone they thought was too fortunate, anyone who had succeeded too well, anyone who had a position, anyone who had a woman, anyone in fact who had anything at all. I asked Pardi what he thought of all this. He said that it wasn't his job to think about it but to narrate the facts and actions of a revolution as accurately as possible.

I carried away the six volumes as fat as telephone directories in which the facts were recorded. Stendhal would have loved this dry narrative, this complete catalogue of human passions. It reminded me of the Saint-Étienne catalogue of arms and bicycles which until 1914 had enchanted thousands of children and teenagers (me among them). Everything there was illustrated, and you could order anything you wanted: a pin to keep a bonnet on your head, or a bicycle, even an elephant hunter's complete equipment. It was "manifold and various" in Montaigne's sense, admittedly, but within the narrow bounds of egotism and self-love (so to speak).

I have never really understood what use it is, for example, to know the details of troop movements at the battle of Valmy. What was it really but a gun without bullets? A mere list of dead men classified by trade or profession: so many dairymen, so many hatters, so many tailors, so many carpenters; a precise description of wounds; a comparative tabular summary of cuckolded husbands before, during, and after the slaughter; an account of the conjugal, domestic, economic problems of hatters, tailors, and carpenters who happened to survive (of the so-called victors, therefore): all these will tell me much more. This is culture in the true sense of the word, for by it I am "improved."

We left Padua at five in the evening. Signor Pardi went part of the way with us, just to the spot in front of Santa Giustina where we had left our car. I stowed my directories of the Revolution very carefully in the vehicle. "Thank you," said Pardi. But for what? Surely I should . . . He was really very charming. He was wearing a black alpaca jacket and a straw boater. He had a little goatee beard. I liked him very much. Then he went back to Padua, where he lived on his own in the Via Bellundi.

We set off at random in the green twilight. We were making for Ferrara. Perhaps we would go on to Bologna. Everything depended on our mood and on the sort of night it might turn out to be. We drove along the smaller minor roads. Our historians had given us a taste for the details on which both happiness and history depend. I was anxious to be in a hotel anywhere, as long as there was a reading lamp and I could lose myself totally in my catalogue of arms and bicycles.

In the meantime, nothing prevented me from enjoying the humanity of a minor road in Italy, as long as it did not lead to sculpture, architecture, and paintings. We were traveling in a flat area, through laden orchards, thickets of green reeds, and cypress hedges. Everywhere we looked, except on the roadway, there were little woods, and the foliage of bushes and trees. Here and there, in the gaps between them, the evening darkness brought the horizon within ten paces of us. But that made it easier to pick out the features of the little farms we were so close to in passing, where daylight's phosphorescent traces still gleamed on the rough-cast walls. On the terrace before his door a peasant had lit a cigarette while his wife was laying the table and the children were still playing. Here someone was lighting an oil lamp under a mulberry tree; there a boy carrying an accordion in a shoulder sling was jumping over an irrigation ditch. At the entry to a hamlet they were erecting the poles and struts of a little open-air theater. Two men were busy nailing up the board over the entrance that would soon bear the tragic mask of invitation. Further on, we overtook a cart full of girls.

We got back on to the main road to Battaglia Terme and passed close to a *castello* entirely in the style of the French eighteenth century. How different from the Villa Ferraroli, which we had seen in Brescia. There they took account of all the lies that a well-born spirit was forced to tell throughout each day; here they had merely dressed to a logical order walls that were designed to harbor moments of delight. Both, it must be admitted, had style. A terrace supported by a rampart and bearing a row of quite mundane orange trees in tubs ran alongside the house; it overlooked the canal. The main body of the building reminded me of Saint Simon's remark about the Duchess of Villeroy: "She was serious, bejeweled, and tall, and, in spite of hips and shoulders set too high, consummately, inimitably majestic. No one could rival her ability to grace parties and balls." You might have thought we were in Austria.

After Monselice we were suddenly in an area of strong winds. The few insignificant hills on our right were now flatter and the trees darker. Wide stretches of ground were covered with dusty vegetation. The road was raised up as if on a dike, so that it overlooked farms as minute as level-crossing keepers' cottages. But you can be happy looking after a railway crossing. Not so here. There was no outward sign of happiness in these houses. But for the smoke rising from the chimneys you would have thought them uninhabited. You cannot think of people without thinking of happiness. What else do they strive for? There is no need to retell the tale of Sardanapalus the Assyrian; there is always a geranium somewhere that someone has planted in an old cooking pot. There is the air that people breathe, and ultimately and finally there is the cigarette that someone is smoking—even if it is made from old butt-ends and rolled in newspaper (and that is often the best because someone has put his or her heart into it!). But here there was nothing. I realize that is a terrible word, but I think it is the only apt one. There were no curtains on the mean windows, and no one had bothered to wipe their grimy panes. No one had lit a lamp, even though it was well into the night. Around the houses there were walls of cement, then of bricks, and these makeshift courtyards were full of ash heaps and old bicycle tires. I wondered what, if anything, these peasants grew. If you care for animals or plants you must soon find some happiness. A pig or a sack full of grain is all it takes. Someone once said (Liszt to Madame d'Agoult, I think): "If neither you nor I are intended to be happy, we must have been created for some higher purpose." That may sound very fine. Below a certain social level, however, you can't live by pride alone, and no one talks like that without actually enjoying more or less all the happiness the world can afford. Then you are in a position to speak with pride and nobility. If you have nothing at all you have to aim so low that fine words and beautiful sentiments mean nothing whatsoever to you. If you stand up and fight, of course, things are very different.

At the beginning of 1848 some very cruel political murders were committed in this area. In general, at times like that people kill to assure the reign of justice and prepare the way for freedom. At the side of the little road to Mantua which crossed ours at right angles, there was a hotel that had been the scene of excesses of pride quite different from Liszt's: the amusements of the nouveaux riches.

Then I saw a little boy of about nine or ten in one of the rubbish-heaped yards. He wasn't playing but staring up at the black sun going down over the beetroot fields. He was the only living soul there. The time for pushing carts was over. Now it was time to light the lamp, read the paper, and smoke a pipe, a cigarette, or even one of those little Tuscan cigars they puffed on under the arches in Brescia. But you can't smoke in the dark, and yet all these houses without exception were in total darkness. There was no one outside apart from the little boy I had just seen. On the other hand, smoke was coming from the chimneys. They were cooking their suppers. But how did they put life into all these meals? I wondered if it was possible to drink a bottle of wine in the dark, or even just to breathe in it without sinister designs. I felt that this was a place teeming with Roundheads ready for the fray and a splendid recruiting ground for some latter-day Cromwell.

I had been told that these peasants worked their land under contract. The sugar refineries gave them the seed and paid for their harvest in advance. Everything to do with their work had been calculated in hard figures, and there were inspectors to look out for. In the long run, arrangements like that can only give rise to hatred.

Even before we crossed the Adige, we felt that this area was dominated by water. We crossed twenty little bridges over canals, streams, and rivers and saw the marshes glitter beneath high rushes. The rule of water was even more obvious after Rovigo. In the open fields we had seen a barge with mast and sails raised. It seemed utterly useless. It was drawn by horses along a canal only twenty centimeters wider than the scow on both sides. I found the mast and sail deployed as if for one of Magellan's voyages most revealing. The bargees' cafés sold an eel stew, but the eels were salted and brought in in barrels.

I keep coming back to 1848. You shouldn't mention ropes in the house where someone was hanged, but it is a period of great interest to me. After the Brescia massacres (which took place on 1 April 1849, but 1848, the Year of Revolutions, is more "atmospheric"), Colonel Favaucourt took refuge in a boatmen's café in the Polesella district. He went quite safely from bar to bar for more than two weeks. All they asked him to do was to wear a bargee's blouse, which he did most willingly. Since he had stopped trimming his beard in the regimental style, there was nothing in particular to identify him. He knew the local dialect, since he was born at Villa Manzana. In the end, he grew so used to the situation that he began to put on weight. The women who made the stew from salted eels passed him on from one to the other, and the boatmen who raised their sails so naively were able to smuggle him on and off their barges. He slept on the boats, on sacks of maize. Eventually they ripped out his guts on some little farm. The peasants weren't on the side of the Austrians hunting everywhere for Favaucourt; in fact, they'd never been anything but against them. One day, they passionately supported the Right; another, the Left. They veered from one to the other not because they were sincere advocates of this cause or that, but because they adored violence. For them, the elimination of this man who couldn't entirely hide a certain freedom of thought, even when speaking the dialect he had adopted as a disguise, was a unique opportunity to *assert themselves*.

The banks of the river Pô were very high. We were quite amazed to hear that it was sometimes swollen to the point of overflowing. In fact, the whole plain was no more than a very broad valley. All the waters from the Alps pour down through this network of ditches, brooks, streams, rivers, and canals, and into the Adriatic. The mountains are not far away: when the snows melt and it rains heavily and continuously in the massifs, the waters descend from the steep slopes and throw themselves with terrible fury into the plain below.

We arrived in Ferrara as the daylight was fading. It was difficult to get through the town at that time in the evening. The streets were crowded to overflowing, and there was also an enormous number (no one knew how they managed it) of men, women, children, and even priests, on bicycles and Vespas. Crowd behavior in the streets of Ferrara was atypical: there was none of the good humor usual in Italy. I saw some very beautiful faces but their owners were consciously unyielding and even exaggerated this hard look. This was clearly a matter of ideology, to judge by the groups of monks and nuns sitting around the newspaper kiosks. At first this was not at all frightening (though they would have been very unhappy if they thought you were not intimidated). You felt the extreme unease of someone watching a blind person unsuccessfully trying to open a tin of sardines with a fountain pen. These people whom nature had intended for a life of sensuality used everyday things in ways quite contrary to their intended functions. They wasted their time and ruined their chances of direct happiness. Later on, you wondered if they were not on the point of rediscovering a very ancient form of sensual enjoyment: one that until very recently people had decided to leave to the devil while seeking the pleasures of human society instead. The present era, I thought, was truly intriguing. You would wound these Ferrarans deeply if you tried to tell them what really made them interesting. What they wanted to be was regicides, all together and all at once. This tendency was so strong that when we got to the Piazza del Castello (where we had to turn to the right), I had the impression that we had suddenly entered a film set where Abel Gance was directing one of his vast tragic epics, and that the makeup artist had gone a little too far with all the extras.

This was another place where they used statistics to arrive at a happiness that was constantly postponed and rescheduled. What is more, they relied on tables worked out by professional statisticians who lived and still live in a cold climate; whereas, with those lips, those eyes, that hair, and those wonderful bodies it would have been easy to follow their own nature and do their own accounting. If I were Signor Togliatti, the Italian Communist leader, I would study the Marquis de Sade to be absolutely sure what might happen when I eventually unleash my subservient troops onto the streets. I rather think he would be wise to count on a vast number of deserters who would start satisfying their desires as quickly as possible, and certainly much more precipitously than any Five-Year Plan would ever recommend.

To keep to the subject of reading, everyone there was obsessed by a series that had just started appearing in the paper. It was about the disputes in some village between the local Communist Party leader and the parish priest. Together, these stories about the Red mayor Peppone and the wily Don Camillo made up a political fairy tale. The author, Giovannino Guareschi, depicted things not as they were, but as they would be if people were really good and miracles actually happened. I thought the series would certainly be a world best-seller if it ever came out in book form, for Guareschi had written it with his eyes closed, pretending that everyone in the world could be really happy and contented.

The motorized, or rather Vespa-ized, priests were rather sadly funny. They were young, full-blooded, and very noisy. They looked capable of dealing with anyone and anything. This was exactly the kind of priest these people needed. They had a really enviable ability to adapt to whatever the crowd in the streets might have in store for them. I developed an immense respect for the philosophy professors in the seminaries that turned out these daredevil divines. You couldn't claim, of course, that the two-stroke engine exactly encouraged humility (though I'm sure that they said the same thing when the first man mounted the first horse, or when they brought out the first sedan chair).

The automobile has done more than the guillotine to get rid of gentlemen and aristocrats. Consummately refined good manners are quite out of the question at a hundred and twenty kilometers an hour. Even the Rights of Man have been overtaken. At five hundred or a thousand kilometers an hour, or at what are already known as interplanetary speeds, the only possible passengers are insects of some kind. But these scooter priests hadn't reached that point. On the other hand, when you came across them on the open highway, their flowing robes looked exactly like the wings of the Victory of Samothrace; there was no resemblance to Saint Bonaventura. Here, when they were stuck alongside us in the middle of a rush-hour crowd, I was able to study these priests' faces at close hand. The only "voices" they ever heard were those of the garage mechanic and reason.

I believe these impressions are singularly lacking in descriptive passages in the style of Chateaubriand. There was a time when I would have enjoyed cleverly orchestrating some theme like "Twilight in Emilia." But nowadays I would gladly surrender all fine writing about natural beauty for a few sentences that really convey the ideal of those who live in Emilia.

I wrote those lines in a hotel room in Bologna. The price, four hundred lire, was on the notice on the wall (and it certainly wasn't worth a centissimo more). But they claimed the real price was twelve hundred lire. At least, that was what I heard from the porter, boot boy, bellboy, general help, and probably much more besides, to judge by the way he spoke to the woman who owned the place. She was thin and dressed like one of Paul Bourget's melodramatic heroines. She was evidently suffering from the difficulties proper to her fifty years of age, with which she was so preoccupied that she scarcely had time for anything else. The boot boy wanted to show that he was a man in spite of his blue apron. I did not deny this in any way and, in fact, I always took care to be very polite to him. But that only made him think he could lord it over me as he liked. He even had the cheek to tell me that on Wednesdays (and this was a Wednesday), and for people "like me," this particular room cost twelve hundred lire. This kind of nonsense never makes me angry but rather playful. I waited until we were alone and then took this lesser Ruy Blas into a very dark corner off the first-floor corridor. I thought the obscurity and cramped space were appropriate, but they made him nervous. He clearly didn't know exactly what was up and how to react. I could see that he was quickly running through a number of possible reasons and suitable ploys. I rapped out (but in as low and conspiratorial way as possible) a long, incomprehensible sentence in which I used the word "popo-lo" at least twice. After these references to the people and the working class, I took out my wallet as if it were the dagger of Caserio, the anarchist assassin, and showed him a number of cards. Among them there was one for a paid-up member of the United Workers' Union (of Manosque) and another one identifying me as a full member of the Associated Benefactors of the Fire Brigade. They worked wonders, especially the second card, which had a picture on it of a fireman in a heroic pose blowing a trumpet most impressively.

In a country of partisans you have to belong to a party—it doesn't matter which—and it is better to invent one rather than stand out as a free and independent human being. In the past, revolutions were made by the people, and for the people. There was a point, at the start, in the naive idea of adopting the aristocratic insult, and calling themselves *sans-culottes:* the real patriots who now wore trousers, not breeches. The revolutions of my grandfather and of my father were like that. I am much closer to the people than some academic of the far Left. I find Béranger, the poet of the people and the Revolution, moving; I know how to laugh. Nowadays, however, the most important thing is to be a hypocrite.

What I really find offensive in this kind of working-class bigotry is that they adopt the manners of the rich and powerful. The workers of the Three Glorious Days of the 1830 Revolution danced behind the barricades and were not impressed by professors: they politely accepted them in their ranks, but as "privates." Nowadays those workers would click their heels and spring to attention at the mere sight of a professor. They would entrust the destiny of their class to people who don't belong to it and would start teaching them to question their own cause. These mentors would lecture them about things which their natural instincts could reveal much more clearly in their true light. Before they have been liberated from their old masters, they are given a bunch of new ones who are of no more use than the old lot. The result is that the workers today can only free themselves through intermediaries: that is, not at all. Consequently, we have all those competing interpretations of the word "freedom" which they are supposed to rack their brains over until they are like chickens in a run who have come across a knife. Because they can't understand the least bit of what they are told is most important for them, they lose all ability to be truly generous. But this is all to the benefit of their leaders, whom the people have set up there above them instead of themselves.

I'm not interested in politics or in the kind of rebellion in which you have to join in with a great crowd of other people and march forward with the masses. I don't like it when some other person comes along and decides to do my work for me. I want to see to it myself. Instead of following the example of the rich, who have become past masters at forming the groups well-equipped to engage in effective forms of hatred, I prefer to make my revolutions all on my own. I'm a shy simpleton who likes to hide away from the world and jump in the water when it starts to rain. The common weal doesn't suit me at all. If you tell me that we are all going to be happy together, I'll run a mile and look for some way of deciding my personal happiness in my own way. In fact, I find happiness in the very act of ensuring that I have it, in doing everything I can to make it happen, and in devoting my life to that supreme task. But this is where the tables of the law, all those schedules and norms, come in. They say how and when I am to be happy. But it is precisely when they tell me I am allowed to be happy that I want to be unhappy. They give me bowls, tennis balls, and part-songs. But I can't play croquet or tennis and my own voice makes me feel sick. But I do like skittles, yet skittles aren't allowed because that's a subversive game. If you start off knocking down skittles you'll finish up overthrowing governments, and so on. Happiness is not a mathematical problem. In a happy world two and two do not always make four for every single person. Anyone who thinks the contrary has no idea what goes to make a human being human more surely than any sultan's scissors.

We drove around Bologna for a while. I was frozen. I just had to go into a café for a couple of brandies. I had caught a cold on our way through Emilia. The alcohol warmed me up and we went off to eat, but I didn't enjoy walking along the streets. We dined off Bologna tripe in a bus driver's café behind San Petronio. This dish (which I'm usually not allowed to eat) was delicious and made life seem more than acceptable again. The café was gloomy and deserted; the little encounter with the boot boy hadn't been particularly enjoyable (when I thought about it), and I was still shivering; but the Bolognese tripe refuted all arguments, philosophical or not.

Elise and I finally went to bed fully dressed in that twelve-hundred-lire bed (reduced to only four hundred) I had heard so much about from the amorous valet. The sheets were suspiciously gray, and we had to put a hand towel (one of our own) over the pillow. In addition, we were forced to supplement the single, very thin cotton sheet with everything we could muster: my jacket, our coats—and I was even tempted to throw my shoes in too to give some sort of weight to the bedcover. It was no joke. I couldn't stop shuddering. But I realized that it wasn't the cold that was making me shiver so much as that gruesome corridor, the foul smell of the staircase, the ugliness of Paul Bourget's heroine down below, and the macho behavior of the boot boy. As soon as I stopped thinking about all that (one of the arts of which I am a supreme master), I was as warm as toast.

What is there to say about a town that you have only seen for two hours at nighttime? More than you might think. The secret is not to pretend that you know it intimately. Some rich inhabitants of Bologna must have loved trees. The last ten kilometers of the Ferarra road passed between a number of vast tree-lined properties. The car headlights revealed great leafy branches on either side. The houses in the Via Independenza, which we had driven along to the city, were superbly matched, and their symmetry reminded me of Turin. There was a slight touch of melancholy and romanticism about it all. It was nine o'clock at night and the northeast wind was icy. The lamps in the Montagnola garden were strung like a constellation overhead. There was an attractive hotel in the Via Independenza. We went in, liked the look of what we saw, and left it because it wasn't in the center of the town. The hotel we ended up in was certainly in the center, but scarcely as pleasing as the first. The historian in Padua told me an anecdote about Bologna:

A factory owner who employed more than two hundred people in his works built them a little sports stadium with a swimming pool, a soccer field, a basketball court, a cycle track, and so on. The wife of one of the workmen, needing money for her family, asked the owner's permission to sell sandwiches and bottles of lemonade from a basket in the stadium. She was a fully paid-up member of the Communist Party, and had six children too. No problem. Eight days later the owner was accused of poisoning the people, and the party newspaper started a collection for the *widows* of three louts who had been sent to hospital with stomachache (and certainly weren't dead, and anyway, by the time I heard the story, had long since been back at work). There was great uproar. Someone even threw a brick through a window of the owner's house. He no longer dared go out and even thought of shaving off his mustache. Before doing so, he asked the woman with the basket to come to see him. With tears in his eyes, he spent a quarter of an hour reminding her of everything he had done for the workers. He couldn't have been more generous. And clearly everyone acknowledged this. The militant sandwich-seller admitted that the lemonade she had sold was manufactured by the rival political party. "You idiot," he shouted, "why on earth did you do that?" She replied— "stupidly"—that she had done it because they asked her to. In spite of his fears, the industrialist was sensible enough to go to the hospital. He found the dead men smoking cigarettes in a little side room. "Irrelevant!" said the head of the medical staff. "People on death row smoke too, and a few minutes later they're just dead meat. So you can't infer anything pertinent from the fact that they're there, still alive and smoking. I am a doctor and, as it happens, head of the medical staff here, and I must tell you frankly that, *if need be*, they've only ten minutes left. Their last moments may be agonizing, and there are ten journalists downstairs who will able to describe them vividly." They called this episode the "Lemonade War." I thought the head doctor's "if need be" was the finest utterance in the history of modern times. He was asked to explain what he meant. He said that Signor X, the factory owner, was too upset to understand what he had intended to say, which was "if it's God's will." I did not find this correction (which wasn't one) reassuring.

Bologna had the most extraordinary of all monuments to the dead. It was ghastly but perfect. Aesthetically speaking, of course, it was zero and even minus twenty, but that wasn't important. It was a wall, probably a wall of the church of San Petronio, with the names of the dead people on it. Each name was illustrated with a photograph—a photograph, that is, supplied by the family. So there they were as their relations liked to think of them: the fat cherub with a handlebar mustache, the handsome, pensive dreamer with a clip-on tie, and all those portraits that composed a photograph album of the obscure. My eyes filled with tears when I read a name with a picture contributed by a mother who was a far from Corneillian heroine, one of a golden-haired boy in short trousers and a sailor's collar. She had wanted to preserve and commemorate him just as he was at that age. I went right up to the photo, both to hide my emotion and to incise that boy's features in my memory. It was even worse than I had thought. It was the portrait of a child making his first Communion, and looking up to heaven. I am scarcely given to sentimentality, but I must say that I was profoundly stirred by that memorial. These ghosts positioned at one of the busiest roadsides in the town and displayed as they were in their humble lifetimes were more moving than all great works of architecture. I had contemplated the columns and chaste vaulting of the most celebrated churches, chapels, and cloisters, but nothing had quickened my faith. Perfection destroys the truly human (which is not perfect, for it has a handlebar mustache). Vézelay Abbey leaves me cold. The souls whom I tend to love or hate do not play the harp. A barrel organ or accordion is much more effective. The grandiose style, a representation of the helmeted, laureled war dead in serried ranks at the very heart of their motherland, fatherland, or whatever (even if that heart is marble), dishonors them, for it shows plainly that *they are not loved*. It betrays a lack of love for that chubby, good-natured cooper who was exactly that when he died; for that bank clerk, for that solicitor's clerk, for that stiff-collared, constipated teacher who died constipated even with an enemy bayonet in his belly. That the people in the streetcars, and automobiles, and walking along the pavement, should be reminded of this was good and proper.

There was a newspaper kiosk beside this splendid monument to the dead. Such negligence was possible only in the country of Machiavelli.

I could think of only one commemorative monument in France that, in emotional terms, could match the one I saw in Bologna, and that was the memorial at La Bédoule, a little village near Marseilles. Quite paradoxically, the French monument had the very slightest hint of Romanesque influence. But it could not be seen from the road that ran three meters away from it. Raised on the embankment was a plain block of stone surmounted by an open book (also in stone) engraved with the names. The mark of genius was first to have placed this memorial in a sheltered spot, yet one where you could sun yourself happily, and then, above all, to have rounded things off with a bench in front of the stone table, just as you might put a chair before a library table bearing, say, a stout volume of Bayle's vast *Historical and Critical Dictionary*. It all seemed to say: "Come on, sit down. Consult this book, and see exactly why we believed or why we were doubtful." These were excellent sentiments. If you sat on the bench (as I did), you saw first the names of the dead, then the countryside that haunted their homesickness, and surely their last agony. The landscape at that spot was not exactly beautiful; the contrary, in fact. But it provoked an intense emotion which the names of the Pont du Gard, the Coliseum, or the Abbey of Thoronet could not summon up.

The avenues and alleys of Bologna were cold when the north wind blew from the Alps. Nothing stopped or softened it as it crossed the plains of Emilia. It reached the city (as on that evening) in pure and simple form. If you added lighting that was the opposite of that in Brescia , there was nothing more lugubrious. When we got there at nine o'clock at night, the men in the street had taken refuge in the cafés where they were talking politics and playing lotto. Now and then the cinema admitted a few well-muffled individuals. The ticket seller was quite shrunken in her glass cage. She didn't look like a cashier busily collecting the takings. She kept her eye on the passersby. When we had finished our plates of Bologna tripe, we found ourselves in a deserted city where the only sound was that of the wind as it sent the big dry leaves (from the plane trees, I suppose) rustling over the stones. Nevertheless, we walked on a little and listened to a clock striking eleven quite melodiously.

In the morning, however, the weather was fine and the sunlight managed to pierce through the great black clouds rushing by to their gathering point in the direction of Florence. I was surprised to discover that Bologna was a sandy-red color. The stone of its houses was what they called Rognes stone in Aix-en-Provence, though here the hue was more emphatic. (Padua was white, for there they used a "cold" stone like the slightly bluish variety quarried in the Lure hills, at the northern exit from Banon.)

We had a minor run-in with the porter-cum-valet when settling the bill. He wanted us to pay through the nose for a weak tea-colored coffee. It was very odd to see how he changed from one to another of his various roles (for he was most versatile). On each occasion, he altered his dress appropriately. He had a cap to bring the bags down; he removed it to go behind the cash desk; when I questioned the price he unbuttoned his uniform so that he could stick his thumbs in his waistcoat armholes; I paid; he did the buttons up again; he

AN ITALIAN JOURNEY

came out from behind the desk; he restored his headgear; he put his apron on; he picked up the luggage. He was virtually alone in the hotel, alone with the heroine out of Paul Bourget's romances who kept watch on us or, rather, kept watch on him through a half-open door. She was in a long lace wraparound, with ribbons and bows reminiscent of Georges Ohnet's late nineteenth-century social novels (especially *Maître de Forges*, or the play from it), and of course Dumas' *Dame aux Camélias*.

The weather was the kind I like: mild and slightly windy. The thick, heavy clouds sped hastily by in the very bright sunlight. We had to decide about the Apennines. We were anxious not to miss them and there were three possible routes. Our choice took us directly into the mountains.

Seven kilometers from Bologna, we entered the Savena valley and Bologna was forgotten. The countryside now was highly talented, so to speak. In particular, it had developed an extraordinary color: a dull bronze that constantly varied its ratio of gold to green. For the first time in my life I discovered that you could use plain colors to arouse the same intellectual avidity that Socrates tried to encourage. Even better (for I am not all that excited by metaphysics), they got the imagination to work. For instance, the cypresses on the terraces of Subbiano, or the vines above Pianoro. The effects of the war were apparent everywhere. The last-named area was partly destroyed, especially the houses along the road, which had been demolished by shells. The bare fragments of wall still standing were entirely ripped and abraded by bullets. Yet these ruins were certainly not sad. People had adapted themselves to them. Once the rubble had been removed, they had patched up a room or two with whatever means were available, and those means indicated a fierce determination to stay alive and to live happily: that is, to ignore the shibboleths that take human misfortunes into account only to move counters about on a board far distant from what really matters. Yes, of course, those people must have been able to claim compensation for war damage. I am a long way from believing in the Noble Savage and even in the noble anything. But clearly they did not trust either politics or the government to see to essentials. They had put geraniums in pots, given the woodwork a lick of paint, and, where the sun went down, placed benches to take a rest on, daydream, and smoke their pipes made from the marble of the old fireplaces. These hovels proclaimed: "We don't give a damn!" And they said it with something of that firm resolution that commands respect everywhere else.

Shortly after Pianoro, we passed a wedding party returning on foot to the hamlet of Zula. The wind raised the bride's skirts, revealing her red stockings. The priest was joking. The bridegroom capered after our car like a kid. The cold wind seemed to have made them all very lively and laughter-prone.

We left the Savena valley and ascended sharply into semi-mountainous country. (I supposed that, all in all, after so many detours and meanderings down below, we must be heading for an altitude of five hundred meters.) It was the light that made you lighthearted. You could see the detail and especially the Pompeian red of the shutters of very white and opulent farms on the hills ten kilometers away. Each of them was a place where you would have liked to live and never care about anything ever again. Of course, you knew that people there had their problems, but, behind those walls with their new rough-cast coats, you imagined peaceful little bedrooms where, with four favorite books, a thousand francs' worth of manuscript paper, a hundred francs' worth of ink, and five francs' worth of new pen nibs, you would be happy. Another source of good cheer was that these mountains never compelled you to any feat of prowess (by which I mean racking your brains for appropriate subtleties). They merely called on you to use your commonsense. If you had some standing or worth of any kind, no one here would know it, but the countryside would assure you that you could be quite straightforwardly happy. In fact, I had reached the point at which that reassurance was welcome. Icarus' complex was all very well but, even after a perfect landing, you hadn't proved very much. It is strange how we are always inclined to push ahead on the human venture, along pathways where each meter stretch has its stone, and accordingly every single step can be marked up to our credit. Yet there are unlimited resources in the curse "Upon thy belly shalt thou go, and dust shalt thou eat all the days of thy life." In my opinion you need more (and a finer form of) courage to be a mason for fifty years than to organize and successfully complete an expedition to the Himalayas. And a more demanding form of courage at that. There is no question of youth or age in choosing one or other of these types of courage; it is a matter rather of the shape of your head. The people who have inhabited the little western headlands of Europe from time immemorial have inherited brainpans that enable them to be happy without ecstasies or prophets.

We arrived at Loïano at a most civilized speed. We were astonished to find that it was a high mountain village with all the appurtenances: long sloping roofs, narrow windows, and the rustic, domestic art practiced by mountain-folk used to withstanding long winter seasons: fretwork, small embellishments, badger hair, dried-flower decorations, and so forth. There were also big, handsome, but rather languid men about who seemed to be playing their parts in slow motion. From time to time I detected a little sparkle in their looks that had nothing of the mountain-dweller about it. There were groups of mules with packs as if at the ready for an ascent above Zermatt. Instinctively, I looked up and found myself searching the sky for some granite projection and for freezing rain. They pointed out, far down in the east, the edge of a snowy crest above an irregular foreground. The bright sunlight dramatically emphasized the shadows, the October sky was packed with black clouds, and everything seemed obedient to the fairly harsh wind. There was a certain almost tragic pathos to it all, yet Monte Nerone was not much more than fifteen hundred meters high.

Notwithstanding all this, the air was delicious and the alpine elements made the houses look like so many toys, reconfirming my desire to stay there with four favorite books, a thousand francs' worth of manuscript paper, and so on.

Since we had been in Italy, we had been playing at buying. Germaine, Elise, Antoine, and I had bought houses, villas, and places everywhere, individually and in common. We already "possessed" (though did not own) a *castello* at Brescia, not to mention the Villa Ferraroli, of course, which we had had to have immediately, ten to twelve palaces in Venice, a tiny derelict chapel in Vicenza, a villa at Verona, a hotel in Padua, the Ca Morosini in Polosella, and, naturally, the Castello Cataio at Battaglia Terme (although perhaps in this case we were forced to sell one of the palaces acquired somewhat thoughtlessly in Venice). That morning, without telling anyone, I had included among my personal holdings seven or eight of those big farms with red Pompeian shutters, especially one that undeniably lorded it with far too great a degree of simple majesty above splendid orchards. I was not sure whether to add one of those houses at Loïano: not a big one, just the little one near the fountain and with such a good view of the valleys of Bibulano.

In any case, there was now the Villa Loup to consider (but I didn't insist; and moderation was advisable). It was the summer residence of Pope Pius VII for some years. He led the life of a contented rural monarch there. They claimed that he read novels, and even that he had been heard, not singing—that would be too much—but humming.

It was at the Villa Loup that Bettino Ricasoli, Carlo Farini, and Marco Minghetti decided the course of Italian unification after the 1859 Revolution. Baron Ricasoli was *gonfalionere*, or mayor, and minister of the interior, at Florence, and had traveled on an ammunition wagon by way of Firenzuola. He was very proud of his sharply waxed mustaches and of a triangular monocle (he had broken his left orbital arch, under the eyebrow, when playing prisoner's base as a boy). Commodore Luigi Farini, Sardinian commissioner and agent of the dukes of Modena and Parma, was fat and good-humored, and suffered from an umbilical hernia. The mountain air made him sweat, so he reduced the sweat by drinking lots of piping hot tea. (This was his very own remedy.) He had a thick voice, and gestured very demonstratively in spite of his short little arms. From the start, whatever the subject under discussion, he was always ready to agree with everyone, but would change sides in the course of an argument, only to move inevitably to a stance of absolutely intransigent opposition by the end. Minghetti, who was minister of the interior in Cavour's ministry of 26 March 1861, minister of the interior in Ricasoli's ministry of 12 June 1861, minister of finance in the Farini ministry of 8 December 1869, and finally chairman of the Council of State of 24

March 1863, was not yet sporting side-whiskers at the Villa Loup in 1859. He had very long, bushy specimens in 1863. He was a modern statesman. Normally, because of Florence and the invention of the special monocle, Ricasoli would have been the Machiavellian member of the trio. But Farini openly played that part. He had to put up with his hernia, and debate was his main pleasure. The three of them had met at Loïano merely to confirm that they agreed about everything, but they were at loggerheads within five seconds and for the rest of their lives, without telling one another or anyone else.

Beyond Loïano the road followed the crest of a mountain chain very closely. There was a superb prospect from both sides. We ascended toward Madonna dei Boschi. The view of Monte-Nerone white with snow on our left improved all the more as we went up. Over it the clouds were engaged in a show of pathos which no one took seriously, but which, if you made an effort, could give you that exquisite sensation of curiosity and sadness felt on days when the weather is breaking up hour by hour. (An Abrahamic tension, so to speak.)

On the right we looked straight down into a fleece of mountains and a tangle of valleys. Some of these mountains and some of these valleys were wild. Others bore or held white farms with red shutters that looked like monasteries, probably because of the cypresses dotted about them and the long, low buildings pierced by little apertures that were merely the sties where they raised the tastiest pigs in Italy.

We entered Tuscany at Filigare. That was where the former frontier ran between the Grand Duchy and Emilia. The old customshouse was still there—the Customs *Palace*, they said. It was an eighteenth-century edifice.

What I fear most of all is that the owner of a fast car should read this book. Fortunately, I am sure that I won't incur this particular danger, for I would be quite devalued in his or her eyes. If the book hasn't already been rejected by such a reader, then this is the point at which it will be laid aside. The whole distance from Loïano to Filigare measures only ten kilometers. If I were to try to describe Italy in ten-kilometer stretches, where would we be?

Nowhere. For us driving was only a practical means of *walking*. We bought all the monuments we liked, as I said, and we stopped the engine twenty times a day to enjoy and compare the properties of different kinds of silence. We would drive back a hundred meters for an archway that we had seen fleetingly and passed already. Nine times out of ten the archway took us to a stairway leading up to a terrace or to a bedroom, and there was a story for us to hear. We never dared to draw Antoine's attention to a goat track that might lead somewhere interesting, for he would be sure to take it and, once on it, stick to it. (He played this game with me one day when we were returning from Nice to Gréoux-les-Bains. He chose the *direct* route via Bargemon-Lagnerose. It took twenty hours. The only people we saw were two cyclists, who were Dutch into the bargain. As we passed one another we laughed at the thought of what awaited them behind us, and they laughed when they thought of what was in store for us behind them. And we couldn't stop and walk, just like that!) We muddled along in this way until we came upon an extraordinarily beautiful pine tree. It stood there, vast and solitary, on a little shelf of shale that projected over the valleys and from which we could look out over the bleak expanse of Emilia. Sun and shade were at work in the plain down below, illuminating villages, farms, rivers, canals, and the rosy-yellow city of Bologna.

This sight was not apparent from the main road. Since our

deviations had been rewarded a hundred, no, a thousand times over, we were constantly guilty of new ones. One of us had only to point out a tree, a lone house, or a wooded thicket, and we were making a minor diversion. Otherwise, we proceeded at walking pace, as slowly as a hunter after quail.

Shortly before the Passo della Raticola, the scenery changed. We were at the highest point of the road, nine hundred and sixty-eight meters above sea level. From the height of this pass we would descend into Tuscany by what we had been told were steep inclines. Moreover, we were facing not only pine trees but an icy fog.

This time, admittedly, we were really in the mountains, but in Byronic style. Uplift and cudgeling our literary brains were superfluous. It was straightforward delight. Everything was provided in an absolutely direct, easily digestible, and nutritive form. There was no Cartesian landscape or Corneillian struggle with the granite. There were holiday chalets (closed at this time of year) and hunting lodges. The chalets and the few patches of pine forest that we could see in the fog were very reminiscent of the Mayerling tragedy, and the strange death of Archduke Rudolf of Hapsburg and Baroness Maria Vetsera in, indeed, a hunting lodge. The doors of the lodges were decorated with *real* antlers. They said that the deer, some of which stood two meters tall, from hoof to antler tip, "haunted" the area. That was sufficient for Antoine to start on a deer hunt, which we had to follow in the car.

I lost face, for my knowledge was far too recent. I had just read on the map that at Pietramala (1500 meters from the height of the pass on the Tuscan side) there was a sight typical of the area and known as the "wood fire." "These are exhalations of hydrogen and protocarbonate which look like a fire." Without thinking, I had read this sentence out without changing a word and so that it sounded like my own statement. "Protocarbonate?" asked Antoine, braking suddenly. "Yes," I replied modestly, "protocarbonate." This meant that we had to stop in the middle of the fog and study the situation. I explained (still very modestly) what it was all about. I had no idea what protocarbonate was, and the haziest of notions about its effects when mixed with hydrogen, but I described a minor blaze in Rome that fortunately came to mind then. Without more ado, we abandoned the deer and set off in search of protocarbonate.

A steep incline soon released us from the fog. We descended into a deep pocket about a kilometer wide that revealed a peasant scene straight out of a painting by Breughel. A man and a donkey were plowing a field. A woman in generous skirts was kneeling down to scratch at the earth of her cottage garden. Three children were walking along hand in hand. A boy with a yoke on his shoulder was carrying two buckets of milk (or of water, but I prefer to think of him carrying milk). Another woman, with her hands on her hips, was watching over her four chickens. A giant of a man bearing a hay fork was striding toward a meadow half-sunk in a little stream. A man in gaiters, a lumber jacket, and a feathered hat called out and signaled to someone with his walking stick. And then, triumph indeed! In five or six places we could see flames emerging from the ground, and smoke. "Just ordinary fires," said Antoine. "No," I said modestly, "that is protocarbonate." We were amazed. We had never seen such good imitations of fires. Without the information on the map (though as yet no one knew that I had read the note on the map), and without my lecturette on protocarbonate, we would have driven unawares past these false flames. "They really look like fires," Antoine remarked. How right he was! We were excited by this quite exceptional phenomenon. I patted myself on the back. Somewhat imprudently (since the thing itself was there in front of us), I decided to risk some more explanatory details, thinking that they would finally confirm the breadth of my knowledge. Unfortunately, when we inspected the flames closely, we realized that they were just fires of grass drying for hay, and that there was no possible doubt that they were this and nothing else.

We passed the turn to Firenzuola. Four hundred meters below, in a gorge of the Santerno, we could see the old fortress, with a sunken road emerging from its walls and disappearing toward the east. This was the road that Machiavelli took to Imola. I imagined him leaving Florence on horseback. He did not take the road over the Futa pass, which we were to follow; it was built only in 1752. He crossed the Sieve at San Piero a Sieve, where there was a wooden bridge in those days, and reached the forested heights of Giogo by way of Scarperia. Some of his proverbial sayings probably originated there: for instance, the observation that the masses are governed more effectively by conciliation than by rigor. I could hear him saying, "Tacitus has already grasped this point," as he rode up these rugged paths, through these lonely woods where the mind alone could raise certain echoes.

Of course, Machiavelli as scrutinized in the Sorbonne has first to be shorn of all his individuality and his body treated with well-proven academic acid of the right kind. I would rather have written sitting under those grim oaks that I could see down there in the valley, then picked up my staff to follow the paths he took. In some of his letters he describes his itineraries, the dates, and even the times. I thought there was much more to be learned by going at the same time, in the same seasons of the year, and along the same pathways, and trying to pursue the same ideas. The mere sight of Firenzuola taught me much more about the medieval Italian republics than all ten volumes on the subject by the Swiss historian Sismondi. To be sure, I have read yesterday's papers. Accordingly, I maintain that it is necessary to try to think like Machiavelli, which is not difficult, for neither people nor those who rule them have changed.

Nevertheless, we are not so free as in earlier centuries. Political parties are better organized, and they come in many varieties. Voltaire would not be allowed to write today. The Voltaires of our times are party men and cheats. We can't even manage to be latter-day Madames de Staël. We must constantly remind ourselves: "You have spoken about people who wear blue shirts, but those who wear blue shirts have their newspapers, banks, their paid liars, and even their assassins. Beware! You speak out because you *like to say what you think,* but they will stop your mouth with your very own words." Yet the human mind and spirit are advanced by what is written with pleasure. The woods that descended from that point to Santerno and all that deep valley of Firenzuola were as black as ink. Perhaps that was the reason for these few disillusioned yet desultory remarks.

We were moving over another pass: the Futa, lower lying than the Raticosa pass but a source of sudden, more vivid pleasure, for it offered a broad, clear panoramic view of Tuscany. The Barberino di Mugello valley was below us. The earth was a golden-black that brought out the whole tonality most wonderfully. The harmony was so near perfection as to force one's rational mind to the same exquisite pitch. Low, gleaming white stone walls supported the terraced olive groves. Faced with these olive trees, so old and wrinkled that they seemed blue, only one—English—word seemed appropriate: *gorgeous*. How different from the olive trees around Grasse! Here you completely forgot how old they were. They were stately giants in the full force of youth. I came from an area of foothills where the olive trees were kept short by constant cutting back, and here for the first time I saw olive trees that brought Homer, Aeschylus, and Sophocles into the reality of our modern world. If anyone in one of those farmhouses lying down there had begun to cry out, I would have thought I heard the voice of Cassandra.

Here all the vines, too, were allowed to grow at will. They clambered up into the trees, so that ladders were needed to pick grapes. They did the same in the Isère Valley, between Grenoble and Montmélian, because there the mountains were so close that they retained the humidity, and the grapes had to spread out in the sparse autumn sun of the region to mature. Vine branches are usually slender and as long as the longest earthworms, but here they were like well-muscled serpents. It would not be strange if the Tuscans were withdrawn and egotistical. To live on a soil that works so enthusiastically for you, and for almost nothing, and constantly to look on such obvious signs of good favor, must surely harden the heart and predispose you to contempt for humankind. All that encourages an agile mind.

I have not mentioned the panorama. I thought of various descriptions that I had read, none of which seemed to have anything in common with the reality. No one had told me that this area was black. The travel agents' brochures and railway posters depicted it as a golden-yellow landscape under a deep blue sky and, since their artists sometimes had certain scruples, they made the hills red. Red, gold, and deep blue are especially enticing colors for most people. I was sure that in this way they attracted many visitors to Tuscany who went there expecting to find a resort like Le Trayas, on the Côte d'Azur. They must have been badly let down when confronted by the passionate *gloom* of that landscape. There was nothing there to please or, above all, *reassure* the vulgar mind. There was nothing predigested or cooked in advance. It was a landscape that Loubet himself, president of France at the turn of the century, for all his facile optimism, would have suspected could never bring in three percent in perpetuity. We were only thirty kilometers from Florence, and the air must have been marvelous in the summer months; yet not a single restaurant owner had dared to open a typical tourist business at the side of this road, though it had a very fine view. This was probably because the view had exactly the same color as the thoughts they were so anxious to conceal from everyone and even from themselves. I burst out laughing at the thought of an intimate little group of four in that place. What chance did you have of getting what you wanted with the usual lies about what fun it would be there with your nice friends?

To some extent, the poster designers who painted Tuscany acknowledged the black (so unattractive) by replacing it with red. They did not go so far as to use the genuine red of Tuscany but that of flags on the fourteenth of July—the red that cries out "Come on down!" like the popular song. The real red is a dark reddish brown, like some old so-called black inks made from buckthorn berries. In comparison, the cypress is the greenest of all trees. There was very little difference between the color of the sky and that of the olive trees: it was like linen tinged with washing blue, though there was slightly more ash gray in the foliage. There was no trace of the crude blue that arouses the pious admiration of sanguine temperaments.

Some people will object that it was the beginning of autumn, and that the sky has a different color in summer. That may be so. Admittedly, the sky was partly obscured that day. But the cold north wind that was blowing, and that was as sharp as the mistral, strenuously set about wiping the entire horizon clean toward the southwest and west. Even in summer, the sky there could not have been brighter, especially in contrast to the dark shadows gathering in the east.

I hate azure blue. There is too much blue in this world. Nothing is more banal than the blue of distant mountains. It is like that melodrama of the eighteen-seventies, *The Two Orphans*. You might weep (if you are capable) the first time you read it, but the second time it's just boring. If that's all you have to feed on, and you possess no bank account worthy of your devotion, you should train to be a math teacher or a customs officer.

In what was surely the direction of Pistoia, the horizon was an ancient, faded-ink color shot through with yellows, shades of red, and patches of violet.

I heard them claim that Tuscany was like the countryside around Aix-en-Provence. It was true that the landscapes in Tuscany and at Aix had certain marked features in common, but the resemblance stopped there. There was a specific attitude of mind in the area about Aix, and in that about Florence too, but it was not the same. When a peasant from Palette or from Luynes had straw in his boots he took his boots off, put on shiny shoes, and went to Marseilles. If he was in with the influential people there, he would take shares in a political paper together with some lawyers, and get himself appointed a deputy. Another would become a businessman and put up gas pumps along the roads. At any rate, he would forget his rough-cast walls, and whoever replaced him would

think the same way and would not spend even fifteen centimes (in 1952 terms) to put his front porch right. That was
obvious.

Similarly, I was not so blind as to suppose that Tuscan peasants differed essentially from peasants in Palette. But a Tuscan's
land did not border on the suburbs of a city with a million
inhabitants which had always been "very up-to-date" because
of all the foreigners who visited it. Venice did not have this
inconvenience because it was a cul-de-sac, so to speak, and its
canals mere toys. In twenty years' time, if there was peace and
the car industry was still forging ahead, Florence would have
all the unfortunate aspects of a modern city subject to fumes
and stress. But its surrounding land and the Arno, which
needed the help of history books to be taken seriously, did
not offer an elevation of the quality of Sainte-Victoire: what
you saw was what you got. Sainte-Victoire, of course, provided something beyond that: a majesty that was far from
banal, whereas the landscape you surveyed from the height of
the Futa pass had retained a certain plainness along with its
nobility.

Now we were descending to an agricultural region. The
vines, olive trees, cabbages, artichokes, alfalfa, and even leeks
were arranged with a Louis Quinze notion of perspective. I
wondered if Cattani, Borgia, Cavalcanti, and Medici Ubaldini
were not varieties of radish. But, shortly before the turning
from San Piero to Sieve, the road passed along a cypress
avenue. I had never seen them so large. Clearly they no longer
had any connection with anyone in particular. They were
respected but abandoned; they were as old as the roads: like
Cagliostro, they seemed to know the secret of everlasting
youth. We stopped. We had only to scale a low wall and we
were in a Dantesque landscape, the most unremitting imagin-

able. Nothing here betrayed a sign of material life. Under these funereal shadows, even the tufts of thyme had a symbolic meaning. The avenue disappeared into a wood of holly oaks. Antoine went back to park the car. We were left to our own adventure. In the middle of the holly thickets we found a grim fifteenth-century building. The people who had drawn up the plans of this fortress were well-acquainted with human ways. They had even provided a spy hole, or judas, that allowed you to inspect entrants to ensure they were your closest allies. The ladies' bedchamber, recognizable by a sensitive note in the forged iron, was perched very high up. A loophole commanded its balcony. Eventually, one by one, the details emerged of a whole defensive system around this susceptible point. It was worthy of Vauban, yet antedated by centuries that seventeenth-century Marshal of France who perfected the defenses of his country's towns and cities. These people, to be sure, had not wanted to be cuckolded, but it was a matter not so much of jealousy as of superb mastery of the art of war. The balcony was a veritable lure. There were two towers. One defended the door; the other suggested desperate measures: it possessed only minute apertures, the first of which opened out fifteen meters above the ground, as if in a lighthouse under constant attack from the waves and with walls that scarcely ever enjoyed good weather. Even very old gardens leave traces, if only aligned box or other trees obeying a certain order, in spite of the growth of suckers. But there was none here. No creature had done more to the forest than a wild boar might have managed. There was merely the cypress avenue, which spoke only of death.

On leaving that enclosure we looked at the market gardeners' fields quite differently. We saw no barrier protecting them, yet there were no plunderers at work. A forgotten bunch of grapes still hung from one of the big vines interwoven with a mulberry tree close to the roadway. No one was there to pluck it.

Finally, from the heights of Pratolino, we saw Florence.

Florence

The stone sealed into the paving of the Piazza della Signoria, at the spot where Savonarola was burned at the stake (don't forget the portrait of this "agitator" in that proud cell at the convent of San Marco), says: "Never promise anything." (The subtext is: "You might have to keep your word!") You wonder how a man with a nose like that, and with those lips, could agree to submit to the ordeal of fire and pass through a burning pile. Never, never agree to walk through the line of fire, except as a last resort.

You should never exaggerate your abilities in front of tradespeople, lest they commence an extraordinarily agile puppet show. Fra Angelico was much more adroit. With his soft colors he worked peacefully, through God, for the ITC (Italian Tourist Company). If you want to see the Florentines of the great historical periods, don't go to the convent of St. Mark, but to St. Mark's church. Don't let the 1780 facade take you in. The interior dates from the time of passionate emotions—the cavernous age, that is.

At first sight, you would think you were in Maxim's, in the Paris of the 1900s, in a technicolor remake by Cecil B. De Mille with rope moldings, profuse draperies, and the gold and the red that excite bulls and aged politicians awaiting their ceremonial robes of state. Here, however, the intention was more proficiently expressed. It was all as if (for why shouldn't I too resort to this useful phrase?) they wanted to establish the myth of the *dead* king and even of the *dismembered* monarch. (This man is a valuable property. All right, let's kill him and then we'll own him forever. If we chop him into bits, he'll deserve all the more honor and a really grandiose setting.) The walls were lit by showcases, for the light was supplied by a whole museum of pink-beribboned exhibits laid out under electric lamps. All these reliquaries contained fingers, teeth, kneecaps, shoulder blades, and even holy viscera.

Before display cabinets like this, of course, you would expect to rub shoulders with a typist wanting a raise, or her boyfriend to be nice to her, and about to deposit her flowery petition in front of a bottled gallbladder, but I was somewhat taken aback to find three women sunk in profoundly contemplative faith in front of the exhibits. You could see men there too, but it was difficult to guess their profession. Some of them were workmen, but for the most part the male devotees looked as if they came from the ranks of those who usually wear a navy-blue suit and whose preferred sign of trade is a tie. The proportion of working-class rather than middle-class enthusiasts was much greater among the women. The three I have already mentioned seemed to be a mother and her two daughters. They were probably stall-holders in the vegetable market. In my whole life I had never seen anything that spoke so eloquently for religion as the attitude and behavior of these three women. Their petition obviously concerned something very important. They were presenting it with enviable nobility, equanimity, and trust.

Perhaps this age of ours, so excessively burdened with human wreckage of every kind, has a favorable future after all. I spent some time beside these quite exceptional women. In order not to disturb them I imitated my neighbors' attitude. It was so easy to simulate devotion that I was inclined to doubt the sincerity of the other people there, whose posture I had copied exactly. You could not stay looking at those anatomical fragments for long without thinking of the macabre operations needed to put them in their emplacements. The dexterities of a special art (and cunning) in its own right had been called on to make the spectators examine their consciences, and above all to scour the innermost recesses of their souls. All those shreds of mummified flesh (in fairly bad condition, it must be said) and bones were adorned with ribbons, lace and frills in the style of Madame Du Barry, the furbelowed favorite of Louis XV. Fingers, teeth, and scraps of jaws were arranged on pink satin pillows. The jars of pickled insides were ensconced in decorative boudoir settings.

People were coming and going all the time without, so it seemed, any precise plan, but as if paying a short visit while just passing by. It all took place on an equal footing, as it were, with the to-and-fro of the street outside. I was drifting into a self-accusatory state, and beginning to share the general mood, when the faces of the people round me caught my attention. They were all of the Quattrocento pure and simple. The oddest thing was that otherwise, if you went to buy some aspirin, for instance, the chemist was just the same as anywhere else, except that he spoke Italian. And if you took a streetcar from the Duomo square you might have been in Marseilles or Toulouse.

A nail in my shoe was annoying me. I went into a cobbler's in the Via de Cerchi. The shoemaker who very obligingly hammered the nail down on his iron last was the spitting image of St. Peter collecting alms in the frescoes in the

Brancacci chapel. Admittedly, the cobbler's workshop was lit by an oil lamp, and there were only twenty-watt bulbs in the San Marco reliquaries.

I was drawn to a crowd in the little square to the left of the post office. I have always believed that it is best to keep out of politics when you are abroad, for it is only too easy to be critical when absolved of all responsibility. So I kept my distance until I was surprised to see no women in the gathering. But the groups of people were quite worked up and appeared to be driven by some passionate emotion. I tested the limits of politeness by standing where I was for more than an hour, trying to find out what it was all about. Since, however, I had not seen any evidence of surges and declines, of that throbbing of the crowd that usually animates even the mildest assembly of conspirators, I finally decided to delve into the mass and see what was up. It was a philately market, with an auction in progress. And there, in the open and in full daylight, as at San Marco, I saw Buondelmontes, Donatis, and Albertis: in short, those warring factions of the Italian Middle Ages, the Guelphs and Ghibellines.

Ardent emotions were essential in Florence, even for driving a nail back into a shoe. The other night Elise and I were wonderfully entertained on a café terrace. Three paces from us there was a fellow of forty or so, who certainly wore a corset to repress his rather stout self, and sported a fitted waistcoat with an emphatically cut-away front, almost clinging trousers, and squeaky patent-leather shoes. (I remembered that when I was a boy there was a period when my father not only exercised his ability as a shoemaker but marketed a powder that actually made shoes squeak. He sold a lot of it at Manosque, and in particular to a blind man from the old people's home who saved his coppers for the purpose.) Our man in the café remained standing up in order to brace his knees, throw out his chest, and make his shoes squeak. He had fine black mustachios, and his behavior made him a cinch for the part of the gypsy violinist they used to show carrying off the princess, the countess, or whomsoever it was from the safety of her royal domain (Chimay, I think), but this one had his own special mad routine. He was rolling his eyes, scowling, snorting, puffing, and blowing, and, but for a somewhat inane expression from time to time (of which he seemed totally unaware), would have been very frightening. There was going to be a concert. People were passing through the rows of tables and chairs: a lot of foreigners, a few Frenchmen, but mainly Englishmen—and English women recognizable by their pale complexions—Germans, male and female, and also some intriguingly dressed Italian women whose makeup was applied with a mathematical exactitude and looked as if they had come straight from their boudoirs. This stream of humanity had to pass at least once in front of the quaint performer, for he had taken up a position at the very center of the main area. Whenever women drew near, and couldn't help brushing against him, he pulled out all the stops. He suddenly became as stiff as a rod, his eyes bulged, and the feigned emotion burgeoned so powerfully that, unless you had interpreted the whole performance as symbolic, you would have been forced to blush on his behalf. Once a woman had passed him, he bent his knees like a cavalryman freeing his thighs from his breeches and top boots on dismounting. Then he went through the same act for the next woman to come by. This game lasted without interruption from nine to eleven at night. He was still at it when we left for our beds.

Those concerts in the Piazza della Repubblica were a great treat for us. They featured a violinist, a clarinetist, a saxophonist, a drummer, and a female and a male singer, all of whom were singularly versatile. I am not exaggerating when I say that they combined their separate tonal qualities with a kind of Mozartian genius. The result was tender, comical, and often more profound than might be supposed. None of them was, as it were, off-key. I don't like modern music, but in this case there was no question of music intent on sounding "meaningful" at any price. These six musicians were no celebrities. They did not pretend to be composers giving master classes as if they were veritable demigods. Yet every night they quite happily devised the raw material for the delight of five hundred people. And I mean *devised*. They arrived, went up to the rostrum, and immediately were quite at home. There was no trace of tedious self-consciousness. They were perfectly natural, and set about playing while all the time remaining their unpretentious, straightforward selves. Everything they had done in the course of the day and everything they wanted to do the next day was subsumed into their music. They modified rhythms and tonality from one moment to the other, adapting it all to whatever they were thinking. It was a conversation between lively minds. They answered, laughed, made witty remarks with their instruments, told one another revealing anecdotes, indulged in asides, confessed this or that, shrieked with pleasure or took umbrage, and from time to time made a very human, very true and thought-provoking point quite plainly. The woman singer (called, I think, Sandonnacci) had a thin, weak voice like, well, almost anyone. What she expressed with total accuracy was what you or I might whistle or hum in the bath. It was the very stuff of life.

The male singer was a theatrical tenor who played the same part in the band as the lyrical element in life. His turn came only once or twice an hour. When he got ready to sing, the people strolling on the square came over and formed a fringe of ecstatic countenances above the boxed spindle trees. He sang Verdi. When he had duly sustained the high C, applause broke out and even irrepressible cries of admiration. As our table was on the side of the arcades, I was able to pick out a uniformed private there who was following the singer most attentively. He had nothing in common with the splendid warriors of Turin. He was very much the ordinary squaddy in fairly grubby battle dress. He was quite clearly there to forget being a soldier for a few minutes at least.

At first sight the Florentines seemed English, compared with the people living in the area between Brescia and Venice. On somewhat closer scrutiny, you could see that their Anglomania was assumed rather than spontaneous. All the same, this tendency was more than a fashionable affectation. It went some way back. Florentine narratives are full of these poker players who remain unmoved by mere emotion but flare up when suffused with true passion. They are "shrewd," so they say, or "diplomatic."

The great mountains of this world, and the sea, the deserts and the lands with cyclones and hurricanes, always have something uniquely interesting to offer the contemplative eye. The Florentine countryside, however, is just straightfor-wardly beautiful. Yet you need variety to lure you out of self-obsession; and even ugliness has a part to play in this respect. When all resources are exhausted, you can always return to the comforts of egotism, or follow one of the many well-tried paths of retreat into self. When the weather was freezing,

Florence could offer three rugby teams, and twenty halls for various forms of physical jerks where you could practice boxing and even judo. But we were there during one of those appalling bouts of summer heat which political parties exploited to great advantage.

You were on the Right or Left, to be sure, as elsewhere, but it was a question not so much of pursuing an ideal as of submitting to the dictates of a certain temperament. Consequently, there were as many right and left wings as there were inhabitants, but no one was neutral. I did not notice anyone paying much attention to what the papers said, or content to follow political keynotes. They told me that people thought their own thoughts even in a really scorching heat wave. Ultimately, of course, they were concerned with themselves. As on D-Day, at times of great social upheaval the public squares and streets were certainly full—but of speculators. I had indeed seen authentic Dantons, Marats, and Robespierres at the stamp-collectors' market. The very same individuals could quite happily transfer their passion to feuds and warfare, and even talk of human happiness for several days, as long as it wasn't raining and they could still wear their hats askew. But, once a particular pleasure had been exhausted (and they were quick to sense this), they would look for another; each for himself or herself. In Florence, classification in accordance with universally recognized values was merely a convenient and superficial way of hiding the truth. The cardinal and theological virtues, together with sins mortal and venial, were the real political parties.

This, of course, was something to be concealed, and where else but under a seemingly cold exterior? As soon as you said this unequivocally, people simulated a politeness that gave the show away directly. They readily assumed a sham benevolence to show that they possessed higher feelings. But you sensed their almost immediate exhaustion by the sheer effort this demanded.

You had to see these Talleyrands when they were not driving buses or carriages, shifting bags in hotels, or serving in restaurants: when, that is, you could be certain they were not looking for tips. What I liked about them was their utter lack of suavity. Vices and virtues alike were sharp and sure, unadulterated and designed for combat (even for what might justly be called street fighting). Some of the people I saw had the most unassuming faith which they employed like a nicked (in fact, double-nicked) bullet. Whenever they aimed, they were right on target. In one-to-one encounters you were lost. Your only hope was to find more than one of them at a time, as they never agreed about anything. They possessed such distinct and forceful personalities that, in spite of all their shrewdness, if they realized you were engaging in some tactical maneuver they would rather give you an opening than miss scoring off their natural allies.

All the foregoing was to be found in the facade of the Pitti Place or the Strozzi. Passionate people are not clever like that. Precisely because I lacked this ingenious mind, they took me seriously and did me the honor of showing to what extent they mistrusted me: even, if need be, to the extent of lowering their guard and disclosing their innermost thoughts. If you spoke to them in the usual Parisian way, they retired behind three-meter thick walls without a single chink up to a height of five meters. Then you wouldn't see even the smiles behind which people anywhere else always try to hide their distrust. You couldn't even talk about the rain or the lovely weather. These, after all, were words to which people gave a thousand different meanings, and which could easily reveal the depths of their heart and get them hanged, or at least allow them to be known, which was just as much to be feared and came to the same thing in the end. If you made an unwontedly acute remark, the person you were addressing would remain quite unruffled and proffer his or her sincere congratulations. If you repeated the supposed insinuation, you would be asked *exactly what* you were getting at, followed by a very cold thirty seconds' silence. If you carried on, you were well into the risk area.

I saw French people quite thwarted as a result. They wanted to shine, whatever the effort involved. This evoked the unvarnished inquiry: "What exactly are you trying to buy with all this?" Of course they were totally deflated. All they wanted to buy was a pleasant evening. But no one believed them. Instead, they seemed all the more dangerous to the locals. Since no one there wanted to take any risks, these French visitors would tell all and sundry that Italians from those parts were dour and standoffish.

That was not the case. But you had to realize something from the start. You could not lean against the fireplace and talk to five people all at once in the hope of interesting each and every one of them. They were such absolute individuals that if you appealed to one of them you would entirely lose the attention of the other four. They had absolutely nothing in common. Even worse than that: you were upsetting their plans. If they were people who were used to meeting together like that, they would all have perfected an extraordinarily complicated strategy that allowed them to spend an hour or two together and simulate whatever had to be simulated. If the one you got some kind of response from showed it, even by a mere wink or a grunt, this meant that by approving or disapproving of something or other he or she had bared his or her soul. The tactics of their peaceful association would have to be worked out all over again. They would all bear you a grudge. It was to avoid that, and therefore out of exquisitely appropriate politeness, that they took no notice whatsoever of what you said and made sure it had no effect on them. Yet, when you were on your own with one of them, if you avoided any battle of wits (which you would certainly lose), and if, as became a foreigner, you didn't stick your nose into what didn't concern you, you could make friends of unusual quality. But you had to be sure to make one friend at a time.

These friends would do everything that friends do. You could ask them for anything, except *their sunlight*, that is, that artificial light which they had manufactured and projected on themselves, and in which they moved and lived like film stars under a spotlight. There was another thing you had to remember: never to try for the limelight. Of course, you could always impress one of them when you were *alone* with him or her. This was even advisable. Thereafter your continued modesty elsewhere would be to your credit. You were in the only place where modesty in close company was suspect, because no one believed in it. They would rather have believed in black light.

All the same, a friend there was more loyal than in countries ruled by logic and reason. Above all, he or she would never be so idiotic as to want you to be perfect, and would like you as much for your faults as for your virtues. If fate stepped on you, such a friend would not waste time criticizing your actions and character, but would enter the fray on your behalf with immense energy and, with the boldest possible claims, defy any aspersions cast on you. This behavior, to be sure, would not be based on the purest of motives, for it would be another way of staying under the spotlight. All the same, a certain risk is involved in trying to shine so effectively, and our Nordic friends are somewhat too prone to shocked modesty when shunning such opportunities. I observed a case in point that was no great public event: just a businessman who had made off with the funds. One of his friends went so far as to find some imaginary pretext on which to attack the accountants who had checked the firm's holdings. He was certain to fail but told me something very like what the Jesuit sings in *The Barber of Seville*: that he would not entirely lose from the affair. Friendship had made him exceptionally cunning. They said he was lucky, but I think he was clever enough to find the one point where the accountants were not wholly unassailable. In fact, though they did not abandon the chase entirely, they toned things down to the extent of coming to an arrangement. Such ready devotion is far from universal. This Florentine who had acquitted himself so adroitly on his friend's behalf said something to me that was both moving and characteristic of his city: "No one from here told you that." I admitted that my informant was a Pisan.

All this was more quintessentially Florentine than the Loggia dei Lanzi and the Ponte Vecchio. There was no romantic melancholy as at Brescia, Verona, or Vicenza, but no laughter either. You couldn't play with this city as you could with Venice. This ancient yet alien realm was inhabited by serious people who set no special value on physical pleasures. Louis XV was inconceivable there. Rather than going into raptures solely before old buildings, I preferred to spend a little time inquiring whether the Florentines sacrificed food to dress, in the way I had observed all the way along the road from Milan to Padua. Was I wrong to think that the answer would be significant for Florence?

We were staying just behind the Palazzo Vecchio, at the angle of the Borgo de' Grechi. I had only to go down the street to find myself directly on the Piazza Santa Croce. It was a residential area. When I was there early in the morning, I watched girls from the typing pool, bank clerks, shop assistants, and accountants on their way to work. In Piedmont and Lombardy they would also be Knights of the Round Table (at the very least). Here, it seemed, they were very different from what they would be in Paris or Marseilles, but what they actually were (that is, what they constantly dreamed of being) was not directly evident. At first sight, they sacrificed nothing for the sake of dress, and looked as if they spent what was necessary on food. I did not see a single chivalrous lover such as Amadis de Gaule, and certainly no mysteriously intriguing woman like Morgan le Fay. I went there fifty times, and fifty times I saw the same people. They began to look on me as a resident. They greeted me in the usual relaxed way, and smiled, but I never found what I was after: a pair of new shoes deliberately worn for the first time on a weekday, an archducal tie, a dashing hat, those little things that make one say: "Ah, you just couldn't resist the temptation, could you! You'll have to go without croissants with your breakfast coffee for two months!" I refer to men here because I always found them more stylish than the women, whom, nevertheless, I did not ignore, though equally in vain.

As far as clothes went, they could have been Parisians. They were soberly dressed, without the least error of taste. The women, indeed, took infinite pains to make sure that they were turned out with exactly the degree of elegance that was called for. It was autumn and almost all of them wore gray suits. It was their faces that told me these men and women came from Florence. I don't mean that they were handsome or beautiful (some of them were very ugly), and might have stepped out of the flattering portraits of centuries past. You saw directly what made them typically Florentine: their attitude to life, their longing to be something other than what they were.

It was simple in Lombardy and Piedmont. Once conceived, notion became reality. "This wide-brimmed hat really suits me. It goes with the shape of my face. It makes me look distinguished (or heroic, or munificent, and so on). If I have the cash *I'll buy it,* and then I shall be distinguished (or heroic, or munificent, and so on). All I need is to look right *for her.* If I just have to have this red tie, this black shirt, these white flannels, well, it's only so that they can make me what I would so like to be instead of what I am. It's well worth going without a little something to eat for the sake of that." Every longing portrayed in romantic novels was to be found on the streets in an immediately identifiable form. And, strange to say (or, at least, strange to me), it did not take much for all these passions, once assumed in the form of dress, to be acted out in real life. I knew a gallant grocer who turned conspirator (and became involved in a dangerous plot that scared the life out of him) because he had a gray cape rather than an overcoat.

In Florence it was not a matter of appearances. Not in the same way, at any rate, for there appearance was a means of concealment. No one wanted to be *summed up.* Lombards, or Lombardo-Venetians, wanted to be taken for something other than they were because they aspired to the exotic; Florentines because they were patriotic. Elsewhere the ordinary had to be hidden; in Tuscany the extraordinary, the essential.

In the evening, when the shop windows shed light on the

passersby, the Via Calzaioli was full of inner storms, and even of conflicts, as nicely balanced as any in Corneille's dilemma-ridden plays: "Shall I buy this pair of shoes that will surely *give me away?* Or shall I keep the secret of my dark heart hidden?"

Elise and I saw something very revealing. It threw light on this taste for conspiracies against the world in general. We had gone to Santa Croce. All at once I noticed a hundred or so women and children gathered around a spectacle of some kind at the end of the central nave, right in front of the altar. As I drew near I saw and heard someone at the center of the circle gesticulating and speaking in loud, angry tones. I was not very used to churches, but I thought this was a place where violence should be alluded to, not become brutally evident. Surely we had happened on some terrible abuse of these sacred precincts.

But then we saw it was nothing of the sort. It was a flock of the faithful receiving the whole truth about sin. These women's faces were bathed in tears. They were suffering acutely, and physically, as if ravaged by a severe attack of communal toothache. We watched them summon all their strength in an attempt to withstand the pain, then succumb to the onslaught before being carried away like the Sabine women. The bewildered children were clinging to their dresses.

I stood on a pew and watched the author of their ravishment at the center of the group. He was a young priest still wearing vestments. Evidently he had just said Mass at the altar and was now preaching a sermon. But instead of joining battle with his foe from the solemn height of the pulpit, he grappled with the Lord of Darkness at street level like any fairground wrestler. He was very direct. His immodest eloquence left no woman in his audience unscathed. Even I was aghast and blushed at his words and actions. For the first time in my life I had observed an actual contest with the Devil, in public at that.

The young priest danced about like a boxer as he showed his audience how to respond to the daily assaults of mortal sin on their virtue. All these women groaned at the thought of their total lack of preparedness and culpable vulnerability. I had never seen people in such a state. After a few minutes of this intensity I felt I was eavesdropping.

Since the priest continued his struggle and his voice rose to a level of anguish proper to the scabrous things he described, we moved on into the Peruzzi Chapel to look at the Giottos. There, anyway, the light was good and we could see everything clearly. A very pleasant scent of vanilla hung about the place. We traced it to a most elegant young lady with a sugared-almond face, smooth and opalescent under her veil. She was talking quietly, though with very bright and lively gestures, to a fat, powdered, well-shaven priest lolling over three-quarters of a pew. The scene was fit (possibly even a little too ripely suggestive) to illustrate an edition of Boccaccio. When I described it to some Florentine friends, they asked if two choir boys had been present. In fact, I had noticed two little boys in cassocks and cottas, and on their best behavior, sitting in the pew and looking at the ceiling. My friends said that meant everything was above board, for if the (obligatory) choir boys had not been there, the scene would indeed have been out of the ordinary.

Behind a pillar of Santa Croce, you passed through a door into a little shop where they sold handmade leather objects. My elder daughter had asked me to go there for a folding umbrella in a red morocco carry-case. A very helpful monk with a very austere face showed me various things, but they weren't quite what I wanted. I wondered what transformation had taken place when, three days later, in a high-class shop in the Via Tornabuoni, I came across the very same man, but dressed like you or me (much better, in fact). It must have been the same person, for, without a word on my part, he offered me the umbrella I was looking for. He had the same eaten-up face, the same voice, the same chicken's neck with large, prominent tendons issuing from the collar of a beautifully soft, light green shirt, with an orange-red tie as the finishing touch, that left me dumbfounded. Strangely enough, all these embellishments quite suited him and his dour Jansenist manner. This was evidence, I concluded, of a particular skill that well deserved investigation.

The Germans had demolished the house and the area where Machiavelli had lived. They did not blow up the Ponte Vecchio, but they destroyed the houses at either end of the bridge, on the two banks of the Arno. The Via Guicciardini was now only a heap of rubble. Machiavelli was born and died at the present No. 16 in this street. In 1469 this No. 16 was No. 1754 of the Via Romana that crossed the Oltr'Arno (left-bank) quarter from the Old Bridge to the gate then known as the Porta Cattolica.

They reassured me as far as the telescopic-umbrella seller was concerned: he wasn't a monk masquerading as a tradesman, but a tradesman got up as a monk. His eremitical face was the result of some illness of the stomach that he had turned to the advantage of his business. He had contrived his agonizing pains in order to look as if he scorned this material world where the rest of us live it up so unthinkingly.

I had long discussions with my friends about the Arno. Jokingly, I had promised fifty lire to whoever would dare to blow up the dam they had placed at the level of the hippodrome. This, it seemed, was a ridiculous idea. I maintained the opposite. In the Arno Valley, on the Incisa side, the Arno was a pleasant stream. Its waters moved with a Poussinesque grace. I had spent some enjoyable hours reading under a willow near those spirited, colorful waves skipping between white rocks. It was a delight, a river with character, essentially of the same nature as the structure of the hills that rose up toward Arezzo. In some places it cast off land and foliage like a woman who, finding it too hot, discards her furs, before it spread its meager yet excitable waters over beds of pale yellow sandstone. Otherwise, conforming to the rules, it played with ruined mills, old bridges, and clumps of trees. It was a river, to be sure, in the sense that it eventually joined the sea, but it was a river in the same way that a cat is a tiger. It was open-hearted, for you could see right through it to the bed it moved over. To judge by the most obvious evidence, its main function was to bring down and disseminate along the valley the varieties of tree that crowned the heights of Pergine and Castiglione. It was the greatest planter of poplars, willows, osiers, cedars, pines, shadberry, and box that I could think of. Liberated from the entrancement of fine words and historical memories, it was a splendid stream that I wished to see running through Florence. There, however, mere words were seductive and the evidence of history could not be ignored. They wanted a river that justified everything for which the Oltr'Arno was thought to stand: the hippodrome barrage which grossly enlarged my stream, and for a kilometer turned it into a shifty, unnatural creature with no connection with the rest of the countryside. They had given it deep, solid embankments fit to take the Mississippi itself, but where dammed-up, stagnant water dozed. You had only to go to the Lung'Arno del Tempio, above the last bridge, to see the living, inspired stream of water I have described arrive with all its peasant generosity, still surrounded by the rocks through which it snaked and quivered, accompanied by radiant trees, only to die a sudden, lugubrious death. From then on, it was the river they had decided it ought to be: that dull expanse near the Uffizi, the Arno as the world knows it.

How much more attractive it would be, I thought, if you could lean out from the watchtowers of Lung'Arno degli Arbeletrieri and survey that clear, living stream leaping among rocks and trees in the very center of the city. If you put a few willows and especially some poplars (as only the Arno can set them—that is to say, slightly askew) in the prospect you had looking upstream from the Ponte Vecchio, all the worthy stones of Florence would rejoice.

There was only one thing wrong with my reasoning: the barrage in question was not modern. You could see it in an old print of 1490. And, when all was said and done, I was there because of Machiavelli and his intimate letters. All the engravings I had seen showed my barrage making the Arno surge back and swelling its waters along the embankments of Florence. Below the dam you could see men fishing with a line and in the water up to their knees, but above it, under the four bridges of the time, the dead water slumbered as it does today. It seemed that they had blocked the water to enjoy building bridges.

I tried to learn things by frequenting places where neither aesthetes nor historians were to be seen. Of course, since I was there as a researcher, I should have been sitting in some secluded library with bundles of documents in front of me. I preferred to go to shops, cafés, and bars where I tried to plumb the mystery of human beings as they are in our own time. People hardly change in five hundred years. Much longer than that is needed to bring about major alterations in the way in which we enjoy life—in, that is, the way we live. The passions are always the same. Experience shows that more time is needed to change the human heart than it took the two front paws to evolve into arms.

In Florence, I noticed, the men who really wanted to be noticed had resplendent haircuts. In general they were young, between thirty and forty, and like Olympian gods with a slight touch of Offenbach. One was introduced to me as a possible source of various items of political information. This did not mean that I was plotting dark designs, for I couldn't care less about politics. I'm interested in the subject only for its dramatic value. Angelo, the hussar in my novel, happened to be living through a period that resembled the modern age in several ways. I wanted to be in a position to see how the machinery really worked, yet I wasn't foolish enough to imagine that this fellow would tell me something that I couldn't glean from the newspapers. I had agreed to meet him so that I could see for myself *exactly how* the political system operated in his particular instance. After all, I was old enough to find out for myself where all the cogs were situated and how they engaged with one another.

My interlocutor (for I played my own minor part in the extremely diverting conversation that began immediately) was in a position (and reputed) to know all the ins and outs of the political Right and Left. For him, there was no mystery to the Podesta or, if you like, the Seignory and the rulers of the street. He knew the Buondelmonti, Amidei, Uberti, and Medici of 1950, the Guelphs and Ghibellines of the nuclear age, and had them at his fingertips. He exercised a certain power or, more precisely, "terror." My Italian forebears prompted me to tell him that he "ruled by terror." He suddenly assumed a (somewhat uneasy) patrician look just as some people look unexpectedly aged after a rude awakening. For just three minutes he was quite flummoxed. He was even sufficiently naive to say: "Let's be *frank*." But he soon recovered. He showed me the twenty or thirty fronts of modern buildings in Florence behind which they not only organized "English tea parties" but plotted the real workings of municipal government at the Town Hall.

I watched him as he spoke. His suit was cut from superb material. It must have been worth the equivalent of thirty days' labor on a production line. He wore jewelery proper to a highwayman: it was both feminine and exaggeratedly masculine. This made him seem banal, but his hairstyle was extraordinary. In his hair, rolled into little loops and fixed with some bear's grease as thick as clay, a comb had described a pattern of checker- and diamond-work reminiscent of black Africa.

I finished all this business and went to *the* fashionable hairdresser. I am pretty hirsute, and my hair generally creeps down over my collar. Usually this evidence of a long-term indifference to hair-styling would have persuaded me to avoid so sacrosanct an establishment, but I had been recommended there, and the appointment had been confirmed for me by telephone. I thought the super-barber would be taken aback when I asked for a mere "crew cut," but not at all. I learned a number of things from him, especially that a crew cut was favored by those who were "really businesslike" but also "reckless"—by "gangsters," in other words. As there is always a touch of Ariosto in Italy (even in Florence), my Figaro took an immediate interest in my head (or rather, as I divined, in what it might contain). A neat little comic dialogue ensued. He had to proceed cautiously before deciding how he ought to direct the conversation. He tried some delicate probing but found my frank and open manner disconcerting. Yet his respect for me increased because I said too much, and much that was too true. From this, he deduced that I used the truth as a mask and that I was very important.

Nevertheless, a crew cut could be a rash choice and, if I had not been so naively veracious, and openly asked questions about things that everyone held it was better not to know, I would have been assumed to be naive indeed. If you adopted this hairstyle, you claimed to know the ropes. They took for granted that you were able to play the game in a particular way. This suited my moderate ambitions. The hairdresser's chairs, positioned with three meters between them to allow people to whisper to one another conveniently, were occupied by men being given an Afro cut. They were wrapped in barber's robes down to their feet. I could see only their heads. They would have made a magnificent portrait gallery for Sismondi's *History of the Italian Republics of the Middle Ages*.

Later on, I wanted to visit some more run-of-the-mill hairdressers, but I had chosen the wrong day, and all the shops were shut. Partly by design, I had a beard of four days' growth, and anyway my electric razor wasn't working. The hotel porter advised me to go to the "Albergo diurno." This was a general service agency. It was located in a basement in the Via Tornabuoni or Vecchietti. There was a lavatory too. You might have thought that was all, but far from it. You could take a shower, or a bath, have a massage, sleep in a bed or armchair, at any hour of the day or night, on any day of the week or year, rent a business office for a few hours, or for a day, or for two days, with all the necessary staff: messenger boy, typist, stenographer, and so forth. All you had to do was to have a very precise idea of what you required (including just wanting to piss) and you were issued with tickets for all your needs.

The typists and stenographers, for example, were in a little room waiting for their clients. You turned up with your ticket and the appropriate number followed you out. She sat down before a typewriter (for which you had to have the right ticket too), and you dictated your personal letters, circulars, anonymous mail, denunciations, the latest prices of stocks and shares. There were even accountants for hire. You could buy tobacco, papers, books, cakes, and, to judge by certain looks from the male and female desk clerks, quite a few under-the-counter things as well. The fact that the whole organization was underground also made it seem somewhat underhand. You expected to find a Black Mass among the services on offer.

You are always kept waiting in Florence, but perhaps it is a city from which we await too much. I took my hairdressing ticket and made for the place in that cavernous enclave where the solemn rite was celebrated. The wall paintings were by an artist who glorified the properties of a certain aperitif in the form of a zebra. The chairs were filled with slumbering shapes. As I passed by, however discreetly, they opened then closed an eye. I was not the one they were waiting for.

There they just turned out barbered heads. Nothing subtle. Just like anywhere else, they suggested: "A short back and sides?" That was the preferred hairstyle of Mr. Molotov, the Soviet Foreign Minister, but I was careful to say nothing.

A coach driver had taken the seat next to me. He was still wearing his very natty uniform jacket and hung an air vice marshal's cap on the hat peg. He started talking to his Figaro. He had driven from Rome by way of Assisi, Perugia, and Arezzo. He put on Parisian airs. That is, he treated Florence as a very backward village. What worried him was the soccer. He wanted to know if the teams would be playing on Sunday, for the weather was rainy. He had his hair styled in what were called "waves," which meant ripples. But they had to be redone as he decided they weren't arranged exactly as he wanted. He explained that his undulating hair (which was long and very black) had to accord (and accord very precisely) with a parting defined by an imaginary line from the bridge of his nose, falling regularly from that curve until it reached the nape of his neck. Eventually he found the right simile: "A windblown look—you know, tousled!"

The artist taking care of me was not at all pleased. Plainly, I was not going to want any waves. Anyway, even if I had wanted them, it was not possible. He was bitterly sorry that he and I were not engaged in a joint search for the right formula. He click-clack-clicked his scissors as a substitute for speech. I have never heard more eloquent scissors: questioning, pushy instruments, they entreated me to reply. I remained impassive. Their sharp little voice was full of childish rage and despair.

Meanwhile, the driver's waves had been successfully shaped. He stood up. He was a handsome fellow anyway. Now he looked like proud Atalanta the huntress prepared for the decisive race: his head was made for speed. His hair artist emitted the usual blarney, brushed him down, and accepted the tip most obsequiously. Now my scissors were silent. From a corner of my eye I saw them poised close to my ear, gaping.

"No, you mustn't!" said the two artisans of the head when they saw the driver take down his air vice marshal's cap.

"As if I would," was the unspoken message of the driver's slightly flexed lips. Cap in hand, he went over to say something suitably jaunty to the girl at the cash desk and, his hair (immovably) windswept, made his exit.

I was "finished" in a hurry.

People there had a great feeling for the comic side of

things. And I don't see why Machiavelli shouldn't be read with an eye to that. He is well-attuned to the farcical aspect of life. Even when enunciating his quite plain principles, he is liable to face stage left as well as right.

I returned to the hotel through an almost deserted Florence. At dusk even the post office arcades seemed too Italian to be true. A quite harsh, icy wind that had risen as dusk came down was blowing on the Piazza della Signoria. I walked about the city for a while. I had never found it more beautiful. Its emptiness and the lamplight revealed its unequaled nobility. At such times you could grasp what Machiavelli wanted to say with his *Prince*: something that applied to the owner of the bar on the corner, to anyone at all, and even to me (if I had been a Florentine). That is why I say that he is not so much democratic as modern: of an age when there is no longer anything hereditary, neither royalty nor riches, neither a title nor even a trade name. Then his principles, which hypocrites term cruel, will be merely commonsense sayings. An authentic modern, like Machiavelli, wants to save time, whereas those who follow John the Good of France, who voluntarily returned to imprisonment in England for honor's sake, are willing to lose it. "Time is money," my Machiavelli might almost have said.

There wasn't even a cat to be seen on the Lung'Arno degli Arbeletrieri, and it was only seven o'clock in the evening. Machiavelli probably walked along this quayside. There are two or three historic dates each year—five or six in troubled times, let us say—that's the most. The rest of the time, that is, three hundred and a few days a year, is life without history, when it's a matter of how to be happy. For my money, it's the most important question of all. What did the capture of Pisa bring Niccolò Machiavelli? Twenty crowns, and countless problems. What interests me is when and how Machiavelli spent his twenty crowns so as to derive the greatest possible pleasure from them. Only if you know that will you know him as he really is.

Say historic things and thereafter people will think of you only as saying historic things. But of course you also said: "I love you," "That's enough," "I've got a headache," "I've got stomachache," "He's a bastard," "If I only had a thousand francs," and so on. They will always think of Bayard, that peerless French knight, placed against a tree and dying with his face to the enemy, reproaching the High Constable of France for the rashness that led to his mortal wound. Bayard was alive before arriving at the foot of that tree, and for him living was the most important thing there was. If we are interested in Bayard, it is the most important thing for us too. After all, it was the only way to become Bayard, and even Bayard as we know him.

From that moment, I didn't give a damn for what Machiavelli says about Italy at the end of *The Prince:* that it needs to be liberated from barbarians, a point which is given such exaggerated importance. Admittedly he said this, but he said a lot of other things too, and he didn't write down a thousandth part of what he said, or of what he thought, and of what his thoughts and words led to. To portray him as continually gnawing his knuckles because of barbarous outrages is rather simplistic—or far too contrived. In fact, he was content to leave us the outlines of a prescription for happiness. After his lifetime academics manufactured pseudo-Machiavellis. Universities do this to make everything as neat as a geometrical Q.E.D. We tend to forget that in Machiavelli's time there was no Machiavelli as we know him, or, rather, as he has been devised for us. Anyway, he said no more than what was in the air at the time. For all I know, having his shoe repaired by a perceptive cobbler (intelligent shoemakers do exist, after all), or a chat with a very sensible grocer on his doorstep, put him on the right path. Then along comes a professor who discovers the cobbler and the grocer and, before you know it, there's another couple of major influences and thesis subjects for source-hunters ad infinitum.

It's no different with Florence, and Venice, and Italy, and our own age. There are ogres to intimidate us on every side. I should have mentioned them to my coach driver when he pointed to the imaginary line extending from the bridge of his nose. I rather think that he would have told me to get lost.

I went to see the Uffizi for the last time. At the end of the gallery I found a tiny room where they were cleaning two little Chardins, portraits of a boy and a girl. Utterly happy, I stayed there looking at them until the restorer returned (he had probably gone for a drink).